Feel Amazing and Look Even Better

Understanding the Happiness Cycle

Anke Mayer

Copyright © 2017 by Anke Mayer

All rights reserved. No portion of this book may be reproduced mechanically, electronically, or by any other means, including photocopying, without permission of the publisher or author except in the case of brief quotations embodied in critical articles and reviews. It is illegal to copy this book, post it to a website, or distribute it by any other means without permission from the publisher or author.

Limits of Liability and Disclaimer of Warranty
The author and publisher shall not be liable for your misuse of the enclosed material. This book is strictly for informational and educational purposes only.

Warning – Disclaimer
The purpose of this book is to educate and entertain. The author and/or publisher do not guarantee that anyone following these techniques, suggestions, tips, ideas, or strategies will become successful. The author and/or publisher shall have neither liability nor responsibility to anyone with respect to any loss or damage caused, or alleged to be caused, directly or indirectly by the information contained in this book.

Medical Disclaimer
The medical or health information in this book is provided as an information resource only, and is not to be used or relied on for any diagnostic or treatment purposes. This information is not intended to be patient education, does not create any patient-physician relationship, and should not be used as a substitute for professional diagnosis and treatment.

ISBN: 978-1-77277-151-0

Published by
10-10-10 Publishing
Markham, ON
Canada

Printed in Canada and the United States of America

Contents

Testimonials	v
Acknowledgements	vii
Foreword	ix
Introduction	xi
Chapter 1: WHAT'S KEEPING YOU FROM FEELING AMAZING AND LOOKING EVEN BETTER?	1
Chapter 2: CAN THESE PROBLEMS BE SOLVED?	23
Chapter 3: RELIEVING STRESS	49
Chapter 4: FEAR AND ANXIETY	67
Chapter 5: BELIEVE IN YOURSELF	77
Chapter 6: WHAT IS AGING YOU?	99
Chapter 7: RELATIONSHIPS	123
Chapter 8: LIFE PURPOSE	133
Chapter 9: WHAT'S GOT LOVE TO DO WITH IT?	141
Chapter 10: WOMEN UNITED FOR CHANGE (WUFC)	145

Testimonials

If you want to make positive changes in your health, wealth, sense of balance and overall happiness, Anke's book is a treasure trove of powerful tips. Thank you, Anke for being such an inspiring leader and bright light in the world, and for showing so many others the pathway to a better life!

Sonia Stringer
Speaker and Mentor to 450,000+ Female Entrepreneurs
www.SavvyNetworkMarketingWomen.com

Anke Mayer is an exceptional woman and a first class human being. Anke is a skilled healer, practitioner and a woman of influence who I am privileged to know and to endorse. Her book Feel Amazing And Look Even Better is a book you deserve to receive and will greatly assist you with your transformation.

Jeffery Combs

This amazing, thoughtful and brilliant read will change your life. Read it now!

Dr. Tony O'Donnell, Phd.

Acknowledgements

This book is dedicated to YOU the reader.

It is also dedicated to my family, friends, co-workers, colleagues, teachers and coaches. Through you I have experienced so much Joy, Happiness, and Love, have learned so many life lessons and have received lots of valuable feedback and advice—all of which has helped me to be the person I am today. You all still inspire me to become the person I am destined to be, should God so will.

Thank you to my mom and my dad in heaven for all your unconditional love and support.

Thank you to my husband of 40 years, whose unwavering love and continuous encouragement is still propelling me forward to set goals I only used to dream about.

Thank you to my son, who tested my strength and patience in various ways. You helped me to realize all that matters in life is LOVE.

Happy people are those who love to grow. – Robin Sharma

Foreword

Anke Mayer walks her talk. She says, "I can help you to feel amazing and look even better." Having met with Anke in person, I know she radiates health and has an abundance of enthusiasm. Anke is also passionate about helping you to achieve real happiness. I found her definition of happiness to be quite profound.

Doing what you love is freedom. Loving what you do is happiness.

When discussing subjects such as stress, goal setting or even the benefits of medicinal herbs, Anke begins with fundamental definitions and discussions. Thankful that she can lead a meaningful and prosperous life, Anke has put together a program designed to help you do the same. She wants you to succeed as she has. She will break everything down for you so that you can achieve your own successes. Her compassion and drive will carry you along if you will allow it.

If you want to get healthy and find fundamental happiness, *Feel Amazing and Look Even Better: Understanding the Happiness Cycle* is the book for you. Although this book is written specifically for women, I found that her book is just as relevant to men. Anke's book will help you improve your relationships, your health and make you look and feel like the powerhouse you can be. This book contains a lot of wisdom and I highly recommend you read it.

Raymond Aaron
New York Times Bestselling Author

Introduction

Life comes in stages or cycles. Once a cycle is completed we have reached a stage that has prepared us for the next round, so that we are constantly evolving, growing our mind, using our past experiences to propel us forward, becoming more confident, self-sufficient and smarter. With each day, each year and each cycle in our life we are becoming a better version of ourselves.

Here, I'm sharing a few examples from my life.

When I was in my mid-twenties my husband and I discovered that we could not have children of our own. We had gone through many different treatments, which in the end became a burden in our relationship, taking away all the fun and happiness of our love life and creating stress we had not anticipated. So we decided to look at other options. We decided to adopt a child.

Two years later we were approved for adoption in our home country of Germany and were told that on average it takes 7 years for adoptive parents to receive a child. We went about life as usual, worked hard in our professions, partied with friends and travelled a lot. I notified my manager at the time so he would have plenty of time to find a replacement for me. Thank goodness I did that so early.

Two weeks later, in December, a caseworker from the local adoption office visited us. Because we were by far the youngest parents among the approved candidates we had been selected as parents of a child to be born later in February. We were full of joy and very surprised it had happened so fast. Christmas was around the corner and my husband had committed to a business trip in early January. We were so grateful for this early Christmas gift and felt we had enough time to prepare for the new family member.

When I came home from work on January 12 I found a note in my mailbox—this was in 1984—and mobile phones had not yet been invented. The note said: "Congratulations! Your son was born today. You can bring him home in 5 days. I'll come by tomorrow afternoon to discuss the details."

I was full of joy and overwhelmed with happiness. At the same time I was not ready for my new baby yet! It seemed the 7 years had turned into several days. My husband was in the USA, the nursery had not been set up yet. I did not have any outfits or a crib; I had nothing but a welcoming heart, great family and amazing friends (as it turned out).

I worked for the next 5 days at my job in our local bank, helping out my boss and my co-workers as best as I could. We lived in a small town with no store to buy anything for a baby. The funny thing is I was not even thinking about that.

My friend Martina drove with me to the hospital to pick up my newborn son. I had to practice how to hold a baby. I also got a crash course from the hospital nurse on how to change diapers and how to bathe a child.

When we got home with the baby from the big city all my friends had set up the guest room in our house as a makeshift nursery with a beautiful family heirloom crib, several outfits, milk bottles, toys and a change table. They also had set up dinner for everybody who wanted to celebrate the birthday of our son. We had a lovely celebration!

This was the greatest blessing and feeling of gratitude I had ever experienced. From one day to the next I became a mom, learning and adjusting to new timelines, priorities and challenges. My life had totally shifted! The friendships I had built were my support system, helping me along the way.

Six years later my husband had the opportunity to work for three years in Canada. Germany's largest software company was looking for someone to set up the consulting services and the training environment in Toronto. I was excited to live in a foreign country, experience a new culture, see new things and meet new people. I was also scared because the last time I spoke English was in high school. My husband would be at work, traveling through North America while I had to look after our son entering school for the first time, manage our finances and household. My support system of friends and family was across the ocean, and I had trouble understanding the difference between the news, the weather report and the commercials on the radio. I was scared to pick up the phone and always hoped it would be a German speaking person I already knew.

I was home-sick yet determined to make the best of my time in Canada. After all, it was only for three years!

The Universe sent me amazing neighbours. They were so patient—listening to my rudimentary English and figuring out what I needed, pointing me in the right directions and inviting us for dinners.

The three years turned into four. English became our son's first language although we were fortunate enough to fly home to Germany twice a year to visit our family.

We all had fallen in love with Canada! However, when my husband was offered a position in management back in Heidelberg, we packed up and moved back to Germany. That is when we three realized that our future was Canada. My husband was very happy with his new job and the new responsibilities it entailed, but he quickly noticed that his family was not as happy as he was. Because of this he made the hardest decision in his professional life. He resigned from the company he had worked for these many years, we sold our belongings and shipped all that was still important to us back to Toronto, where we planned to start our own business and a new life abroad.

Without these experiences in my life I would have never attempted such a crazy new adventure.

Why would we leave our familiar support system (friends and family and financial security) again and start something we had never done before in a foreign country? The answer is we followed our heart and we trusted that it would somehow work out. We trusted in our talents and strength to support each other and anticipated finding the right people to become successful. We helped others on a similar journey to advance their skills and bring their families to a safe and free country.

Life prepares us for what lies ahead and brings other people into our life, who help us make it all happen. All we need to do is trust in ourselves, do the best we can, be open to other people, continue learning and be grateful for how far we have come.

Even at the wonderful age of 84 my mother is still learning and working on her mobility, strength, patience and more.

Five years ago when she was going for an evening walk with a friend and her dog, she stumbled, fell and broke her hip. After a successful surgery to replace her hip she fell into a coma for several days, and when she woke up she could no longer talk, swallow, walk or move her limbs.

Instead of accepting her fate, she worked hard with the rehab made available to her so she could be transferred into a care facility for the elderly. Once there she continued to work at improving her physical disabilities. Two years ago she was the first person to move out of that facility into her own apartment. She still needs some care but she has gained back her independence.

One of the lessons I learned over the first 55 years of my life is that we are in control of the choices we make but after that we have to be willing to adjust our way to the circumstances that present themselves and be open to change. We are not always in control of the small stuff yet will achieve what really matters in our life. I look at the obstacles and challenges as tests we have to pass to prove how serious we are about our important goals.

As Rod Hairston—a successful and sought-after coach for management of top fortune 500 companies—puts it, "What you focus on you find, what you focus on grows, what you focus on seems real, and what you focus on ultimately you become."[1]

We are designed to become better in growing as a human being, so let's shine and inspire others to shine, too.

[1]Rod Hairston: http://www.envision-u.com/pr/team.asp

Feel Amazing and Look Even Better

Ways To Live A Better Life:

STOP

Playing The Victim Card
Making Excuses
Letting Others Tell You How To Live
Trying To Make Others Happy
Doubting Yourself

START

Spending More Time Outside
Thinking Positive
Believing In Yourself
Creating Your Own Happiness
Making Your Dreams, Desires
& Wishes Happen

Chapter 1

WHAT'S KEEPING YOU FROM FEELING AMAZING AND LOOKING EVEN BETTER?

Over the past 60 years the role of women in western society has dramatically changed. Compared to most women in less developed parts of the world, today's woman has access to education, health care, transportation, clean water and food. But … with these privileges also come higher expectations that we have for ourselves and that society has about us. We feel not only obligated to care for our family and loved ones but are compelled to use our education and contribute to the family income, our church, our community, the greater good and still look good and feel amazing. That's a tall order.

Since the arrival of the Internet and social media, technology has evolved to a huge extent. Now we have access to news around the world in an instant. With the introduction of the smartphone we can reach others and can be reached by others wherever we are. Many people can even work from home in their profession because of advancement in technology. For the most part all they need is a phone and access to the Internet to be productive. But as much as all this advancement adds convenience to our life, it also requires us to adapt rapidly.

We all know that the day has 24 hours. Eight hours or more are spent at the office or, if you work from home, at your desk. The commute in most cities today is between one and two hours one way, which adds more hours to your day. Most women still tend to their household chores: the kids have to be picked up from school or day care, they help with homework, shop, prepare meals, clean and wash, and then there is quality time to be scheduled with the family. Driving the kids to after school programs and sports events rounds out the day in many families. Many of you also care for older family members, neighbours or friends.

In my line of business I meet more and more young, ambitious and entrepreneurial women who want to decide when they are working, how many hours they want to work and who they want to work with. Time freedom is the new paradigm. This new vision and the reality that more jobs are reduced, moved or cut altogether is transforming the way many of us will pursue our career and earn an income in the decades to come.

But if you still work outside your house for a boss who dictates your time, hours worked, your pay, time off, where you have to work and who you have to work with, stress has become a major health risk. It makes it so much harder to have fun at work. It becomes even worse when you get paid less than what you actually deserve. Finding any me time to recharge the battery seems almost impossible. Fear and anxiety only add to the problem, with more and more companies outsourcing services to other countries, downsizing or shutting down all together. In most cases the family depends on your income. Many of you are also single moms. In fact, financial stress is one of the main reasons for divorce.

It is very hard to stay confident in your own abilities if you have experienced a job loss, a separation or a divorce—or even the loss of a significant person in your life. You may be scared, wondering how you can manage. The older you get the harder it will be to find new employment. The older you get the harder it will be to remain healthy, flexible and adjust to change, stay sharp in your mind and attractive to your partner. Many physical changes are also happening as we get older.

Stress and age contribute to hormonal imbalances that impact the way we feel and look. In short, our skin and flesh sags, the belly bulges and we feel a constant lack of energy to go about our daily routine. How in the world can we be happy about that?

With a lot of stress, a less attractive body, low energy and self-esteem many partnerships are suffering too. Did you know that just about 50% of all marriages end in divorce? (See this informative piece at: http://www.dailyinfographic.com/divorce-in-america-infographic)

Do you feel that your busy life is giving you less opportunity to do the things you truly enjoy? Things like taking care of yourself by

Feel Amazing and Look Even Better

sleeping in on the weekend, getting a manicure or a pedicure, having your hair done, arranging a massage, running away for a Spa Day or even going out for dinner and a movie may just not cross your mind. Maybe you struggle financially, too, so these luxuries are out of the question.

You used to have hobbies and enjoy the things you love and are good at. Maybe you're passionate about causes for the greater good like the environment, animal rights or people rights but can't find the time to act on these feelings. You long to hang out with friends to just have fun with and to be the person you really are. You no longer day-dream to calm down and to connect with your inner self so as to plan for and lay out your wildest dreams and goals. And who in all this chaos still has time to work out to stay fit?

Well, you aren't imagining things. Americans, in general, don't get time off and they don't take paid holidays. Canadians are luckier: we get one day off per week and do alright for paid annual leave. Australians are another group of people who don't get time off every week, but they compensate with more paid leave. The statistics are appalling.

Want to know why people are so stressed? Take a look at the charts on the follow pages!

Balancing family and a career

You feel obligated to balance everybody else's needs before your own because you love harmony and feel others' needs are more important than your own.

Of course the kids need you first and foremost because you want to make sure they are safe, stay healthy and grow up with all their needs taken care of. You want to make sure you make NO mistakes so they can become the successful, confident and independent people you envision. The kids want to play sports, a musical instrument, dance, perform or need a special school. They need you to help prepare for and bring them to their practices and events.

You also love your spouse. He or she needs attention from you. They don't exist in a vacuum, so you listen to their problems and their stresses

Feel Amazing and Look Even Better

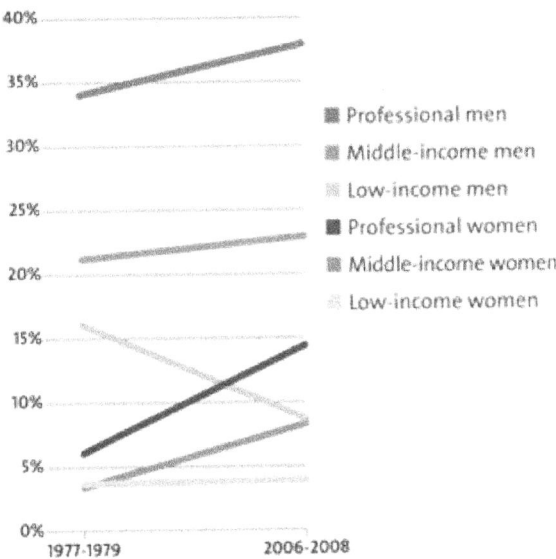

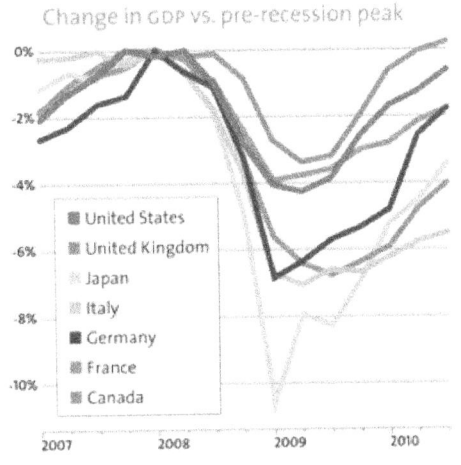

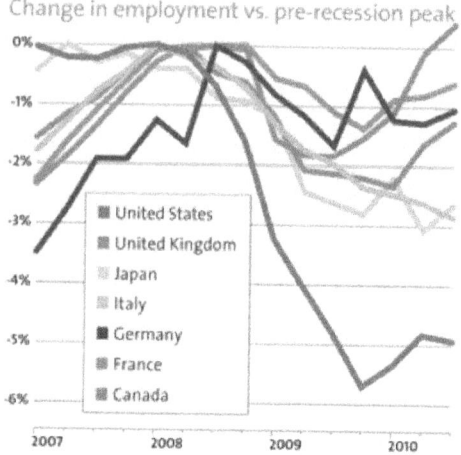

and try to help them be happy so they also feel appreciated and remain passionate about you.

If you live in a partnership, household chores and shopping can be shared. But who has the time to always prepare healthy meal options? Single moms most often have to do it all alone!

Your parents and other older family members may rely on you for ongoing support to run errands, help them with chores, look after their finances and invite them to dinners or parties to make them feel good and appreciated. Because you are younger and often fitter than them. you want to help out too. They took care of you when you were little. You love them and want them to feel good as they get older.

And then there are the following situations that escalate the problem immensely: the fact that more adult children are living with parents and more elderly parents are living with adult children. Try adding these realities into the balance!

Census data from Seattle in 2008 showed a record number of elderly parents are now living with their adult children. In the previous seven years, the number surged by 62 percent.

The preceding graphics originate at http://www.motherjones.com/

Higher housing costs, the economy and the cost of medical care all play a role in the trend. And caring for an elderly parent isn't easy, especially when you're trying to hold a job. Forty percent of caregivers who work full-time report missing work on a regular basis as they try and meet the needs of an elderly loved one.

According to U.S. Census Bureau data, 2.3 million elderly parents were living with their kids in the year 2000. And by 2007 the number had jumped to 3.6 million.[2]

UNITED STATES (Record levels of young adults living at home, says ONS) - Stricter mortgage criteria and rising rents, coupled with higher unemployment, means more young adults are staying in the family home, official figures show.

Between April and June 2013, 19% of the economically active population aged 18-24 was unemployed.

The number of young adults living with their parents has increased by a quarter since 1996, official figures show, with high house prices and growing youth unemployment forcing many to remain in the family home.

A total of 3.3 million 20- to 34-year-olds lived with their parents in 2013, according to the Office for National Statistics, the highest number since it started keeping records in 1996.

Over that period the number of young adults sharing a home with their parents rose by 25%, despite the proportion of the population aged between 20 and 34 remaining broadly the same.

The ONS data showed that people were most likely to live with their parents in their early 20s, with 49% of 20- to 24-year-olds in the family home, compared to 21% of 25- to 29-year-olds, and 8% of 34-year-olds – and it is the percentage of the youngest age group that has increased most noticeably, rising from 42% in 2008.

Young adults have been hit hardest by unemployment in the downturn, and the figures suggest this has been a factor behind increasing numbers staying in the family home. Between April and June 2008, 13% of the economically active population aged 18-24 was unemployed, a figure that had increased to 19% by the same period of 2013.

The percentage of unemployed people who live with their parents (13%) is more than twice that (6%) of those who live independently.

The increase in the number of young adults living with parents also coincides with a period in which house prices rose relative to incomes. In 1996, the typical first-time buyer had to raise 2.7 times their salary to afford to buy a home, but by 2013 the figure stood at 4.47. This, combined with stricter mortgage criteria and rising private rents, is likely to have driven more young adults back to the family home.

Matthew Pointon, housing economist at Capital Economics, said it was no surprise the increase had coincided with the economic downturn.

"The recession hit the young particularly hard, with a sharp rise in youth unemployment. Furthermore, there was a collapse in the availability of mortgages for buyers with small deposits, which prevented many would-be first-time buyers from flying the nest," he said. "With lenders demanding a deposit of at least 25%, and with savings rates at record lows, many young buyers desperate to get on the housing ladder would have seen staying with their parents a little longer to boost their savings as their only option."

Many young adults are trying to save the cost of living on campus and opt for living at home instead. With student loans at record heights, many see no other option.[3]

"Canadians are making sacrifices to prepare themselves for a changing workforce. Federal and provincial government decisions are forcing students to take on more education-related debt than any previous generation, while middle class earnings have largely stagnated in the past twenty years.

Skyrocketing tuition fees and the prevalence of loan-based financial assistance have pushed student debt to historic levels. This past year, almost 425,000 students were forced to borrow in order to finance their education. The aggregate of loans disbursed by the Canada Student Loans Program, less the aggregate of loan repayments received is resulting in student debt increasing by $1 million per day."[4]

In the US the figures are not much different. A recent report from the New York Fed states "Between 2004 and 2012, the number of borrowers increased by 70% from 23 million borrowers to 39 million. In the same period, average debt per borrower also increased by 70%, from about $15,000 to $25,000."[5]

Christine Northam, a counsellor at the advice charity Relate, said the change was also putting pressure on parents who had expected their children to move out when they went into higher education. "It's a role change, people may have to learn to cope with living with an adult child. If the couple aren't very good at adapting it can be difficult," she said. "Couples who had held on for the sake of the children find that they are holding on for longer."

A breakdown of the figures along gender lines showed that for every 10 women aged 20-34 who lived with their parents in 2013, 17 men did so.

"In the 20-34 age group, over 600,000 more women than men were living as part of a couple in their own household," it said. "The main reason for this is that, on average, women form partnerships with men older than themselves. Thus more women than men in this age group were married or cohabiting."

In addition, 589,000 more women than men were lone parents in their own household, and women were more likely to take part in higher education than men, leaving the family home to do so.

The ONS (Office of National Statistics) also compared UK data with figures from Europe, and said that in many EU countries young adults were more likely to live with their parents.

Financial stress and lack of job security

Your lifestyle and financial obligations make it necessary for both partners to contribute financially to the family income. Those with a college or university education carry student loans, which can never be forgiven and have to be paid back.[6][7]

Once you have children you need larger apartments or homes that usually carry a mortgage.

Maybe you are in a career you very much enjoy. But that also requires a safe and well-run day care, which in turn costs money, too. The kids need new clothing and shoes twice per year, as well as toys and

extra-curricular activities to foster their talents and develop their self-confidence.

While at work you are balancing company politics, supporting co-workers to finish projects in time, pleasing your boss to keep the career options open and managing to not get fired.

Did you know that only 16% of us work in our dream job? This means you are likely to be frustrated about the work you are doing daily, battling traffic to get there in time, feeling unappreciated, underpaid and/or overworked. At the same time more and more companies are reducing hours or offering contract work rather than employment, where regular hours and your paycheck can be cut at any time. Or, perhaps, you have to work more hours to make ends meet or meet expectations. Social media has become part of your life, too, and you may be required to carry a pager or smart phone so you can be reached at all hours of the day. You are expected to respond to e-mails and texts immediately and answer the call of the boss or clients at any time.

May 20, 2015: The International Labour Organization says only 25% of workers around the world have permanent jobs.[8]

Environmental stress: toxicity, noise and radiation

In today's world we are exposed to toxins all around us. In the air we breathe, the water we drink, the food we eat, the personal care products we use and even the clothes we wear. There is no way of escaping the ever-increasing toxicity in our environment. Environmental toxicity and free radicals are known to take a toll on your body, often in the form of low energy, fatigue and visible signs of premature aging.[9][10] Also, indoor air pollution can affect you at home, work, or even places you visit. It can increase your risk of a respiratory disease, such as asthma, allergies, and lung cancer. Indoor air pollution can be worse in winter, when windows are shut tight and less fresh air can circulate. A study found that three pollutants commonly found in houses have the greatest effect on health:

- Formaldehyde, which is released mainly by building materials.
- Acrolein, which comes from heating cooking oil to high temperatures and from cigarette smoke.
- Tiny particles called respirable particulates that can get into the lungs. A common source of respirable particulates is tobacco smoke.

Many toxins are found in the furniture, the carpet or flooring, other building materials, paint, upholstery and mattresses, fabrics. Ventilating your home daily will help to some extent. It does not eliminate them.[11]

Prescription drugs, and pesticides are found in our water supply. Hormones are found in the meat we eat. They encourage faster growth of life stock and thus more profits for industry.

Paraben and Phthalates of different kinds and variations are found in most of the personal care products we use. They make plastics soft, keep the product smell nice and last longer. Our skin is the largest organ and we absorb these toxins with every bath or shower we take.[12]

There is no way any of us can escape the daily toxic overload. More and more chemicals are introduced into the food chain, personal products, your clothing, carpets, furniture, building materials, household items etc. Prescription drugs are increasingly showing up in the water supply and pollutants are part of the air breathe.

Hormones and antibiotics are showing up in the meat we eat.

Through the choices we make every day and with the habits we develop we have a way of influence and industry has already adjusted to the demands of the consumer. These days we find more options for clean organic products than even 10 years ago: using more natural household cleaners and air fresheners, eating clean organic non genetically modified food, drinking filtered water, recycling our leftover prescription drugs and household cleaners and chemicals properly and not flushing them down the toilet or drain. There is a lot we all can do to promote change and reduce toxic stress on the body.

Regular detoxification of the body is another way to stay healthy and reduce the stress these chemicals put on our body and the way we feel. To maintain good health we have to cleanse out impurities and toxins regularly. I use Nutritional Cleansing. It works on a cellular level and supports the liver and kidney function. This is a great way of housekeeping. Just think about it. If your house or car falls apart and cannot be repaired you can buy another one. But your body is the only one you have in your life. Replacing or repairing any parts is costly and has risks. Why not take great care of it while you can?

Obesity is on the rise worldwide, even among children. Recent studies found a link between toxicity and weight gain or increase of visceral fat. To protect vital organs from the increase of toxins the liver stores the toxins in visceral fat around your inner organs. That is why more and more people increase around their belt line.[13][14]

A great source for safe personal care products

A great source for safe personal care products (http://www.ewg.org/skindeep/) and clean food sources is the nongovernmental Environmental Working Group (EWG), (http://www.ewg.org/foodnews/).

What foods are important to reduce the stress on our body and maintain good health?

We have always been told by our parents to eat our veggies to stay healthy. An apple a day keeps the doctor away. But these strategies do not help to the same extend as they did even 25 years ago. The food industry has changed and so has our life-style.

- Governments reward farmers with subsidies and tax breaks when they achieve certain quotas.
- GMOs (Genetically Modified Organisms) were created to provide us with food that looks great, is more tolerant to environmental conditions, has a longer shelf life and requires fewer pesticides. But Nature has adjusted and now farmers have to apply many times more pesticides to those GMO seeds (that already have a strain of pesticide in their gene) to allow for maximum harvest.
- Our farmers in warmer climates have advanced their industry to harvest multiple times per year without giving the soil the natural ability to recuperate and transform any natural fertilizer into inorganic matter that can be uptaken by the plants and then absorbed by our body when we eat them. Instead they use chemical fertilizers to grow their produce faster. Our food has become nutrient deficient in trace minerals which are essential to our health.

- What does that mean for us? Our food is not as nutritious and nutrient rich as 20 years ago. To get the same nutritional values out of today's spinach you need to eat almost twenty times as much as 20 years ago.[15]

I have opted to participate in local CSA programs.[16]

I get to know the farmer and can find out how he grows the produce or livestock and whether the seeds are non-GMO and what the livestock is fed. This program also allows me to support local ethical and environmentally responsible farming.

With the increase of electronic devices you are exposed to radiation daily, which can have an impact on your health, according to several studies.

The denser the community you live in, the smaller your living space becomes and the higher the noise level will be from Video games, TV, radio. Your mind has less and less ability to relax and shrug off the effects of stress. Living in a virtual world can be fun and make things easier, or not. Access to electronic devices like smart or mobile phones not only let us connect instantly. It also makes us available 24/7. Do you feel you still have to be available after hours? Does your employer expect you to respond to calls, texts or email messages long after you left the office?[17]

Today's answer to stress can be found in numerous ways.
- Being out in nature for sports and fun. Through physical activity you can release stress simply by going for a brisk walk outside.
- Participate regularly in a fitness class and make physical fitness part of your lifestyle.
- Through proper nutrition you are able to reduce toxicity in the body and balance your cortisol level. While some stress may be healthy in that it helps you to accomplish more, challenge yourself and help you reach new goals or personal bests, constant or chronic stress can be harmful and may even lead to depression and other health problems.
- Through mindfulness, meditation and visualization.
- Listening to music.

Fear and anxiety

Instant news informs you about many disasters, accidents, war fatalities and crimes, not only in your neighbourhood, community or country but around the world. You are exposed to negativity and bad news 24/7.

You are scared and afraid for your children, your family and your friends, always thinking "What if something like this is happens to us?" Or you may feel overwhelmed at not being able to help the way you would like to.

You also fear that you are not enough, that you are not living up to other people's expectations.

You wonder if your partner still loves you the way you are. Your skin is sagging; you may have gained a few pounds from having had children or getting older. Your hair is getting grey and your skin wrinkly. Romance is lacking because you are constantly tied-up or thinking about your schedule—so as not to miss anything.

Lack of belief in yourself

Do you feel comfortable about your abilities and strengths? Have you been successful in your endeavors so far? How confident are you to make things happen?

Do you feel appreciated at work, loved by your partner and your family? How do you think and talk about yourself? Do you care what others think of you?

Do you love who you are, how you look and feel?

Premature aging

Aging starts in your thirties. Some people get frustrated about the first grey hair or wrinkle around the eyes or mouth. It is part of life that we get older. The increase of toxicity in your environment, the lack of nutrition in your diet, and the impact of constant stress in your life has an impact on you and the way you age. Can you do something to slow this process down? You see more and more people around you getting sick, developing debilitating conditions, in need of artificial joints, developing a compromised immune system, allergies of all kinds, heart conditions, a fading mind, etc. You want to live longer and be able to maintain independence and a good quality of life at the same time. Is that possible, and what can you do to lay a solid foundation for good health and slow down premature aging?

Struggling with relationships

There are so many things you want to do, have to do and feel obligated to do; for instance, helping out in your community or church—on top of everything else already mentioned. The thing is, the day only has 24 hours and you feel you run out of time every day. Do you have to do all the work on your own? Who can you turn to for support?

Relationships are becoming more and more important to share the burden. "I help you and you help me" is the first step. "Let's do it together" is the next one.

Being part of a community or group of like-minded people provides a sense of belonging where ideas can be discussed, fun and sadness are shared and you are valued for your contributions and traits. I am part of a community of women who support each other if needed and have fun in various ways. Check us out at www.SociableSisters.com.

Are you a positive person who is attracting positive like-minded people into your network? Are you living by example, being open, honest and authentic? How can you improve your network and get more done in less time?

No sense of purpose

Why are you here? Have you ever asked yourself this question? Maybe you never thought about it because you never took the time.

Did you ever feel you'd love to do something because it makes you feel good doing it—or because you are actually good at it? Are you really enjoying what you do and never worried about how much time and effort it takes? How excited and passionate are you about your work? Maybe your work also has a positive impact on others either directly or indirectly. Do you feel compelled to achieve because it makes you feel great? Your pay may even become secondary because you feel driven to do what you want to do.

Why is all that important at all? How will this affect your current dilemma?

No love

They say "Love Makes the World Go Round." Really?

What does that mean? Why is that so? How does that matter in your life? What will change?

Some people feel they no longer trust in love. Maybe you've been disappointed, or you've never experienced it at all.

Some people may mix up love with sex.

Are there different types of love? What difference will love make in your life?

No participation

Many people are turning away from problems that affect our society here and in other countries around the world. Are you aware that your actions or the lack of them not only impacts how your life unfolds, but your participation and support of causes, initiatives and ideas also impacts others? Our attitude towards, respect for, and interest in others shapes our environment, the way we feel and how others feel about us. We all have the opportunity to create positive change for ourselves, the people we care about or the common good.

This is WHY I do what I do in my professional and my private life. I have always looked for ways to have a real impact on people's lives in a positive way. Empowering others to do well creates a strong sustainable base for financial independence and lasting change. Education and cooperation in the pursuit of a common goal where we leverage each other's efforts, knowledge and expertise for a greater and growing impact is what I am passionate about. When people get the chance to use their own skills and abilities, are able to support each other and create a future they are proud of, they have an opportunity for happiness. As Robin Sharma puts it "Happy people are those who love to grow."

The fact that I have the opportunity to live a meaningful and prosperous life while others struggle to survive has always kept me looking for a solution. While I cannot help everybody, I know that as a group we can help many more, and create a ripple effect through education, training and support to lift up many more people's lives, to create a movement where others can join in. It's why I started my new business, why I wrote this book and it's why I began the charity listed directly below.

WUFC (Women United for Change)

What is "Women United for Change"? We are a movement, led by women from across the network marketing / direct sales profession. By building our own businesses, we have become empowered (personally, professionally, spiritually and financially). We want to help other women experience the amazing transformation that comes about by having a business (particularly those in the poorest countries in the world). Since founding WUFC in March 2015 we are supporting more than 1,600 women to start their own business using their unique skills and resources, monitoring their progress for adjustments, and teaching them leadership skills to lift up their communities by teaching others the same.

We know that by investing a small portion of the profits from our network marketing/direct sales businesses into the Women Empowered program, we're making a big difference in the lives of other women (and for the world at large). And that's why we've partnered with PCI's *Women Empowered Program* and how we're helping women in developing countries.

Women United for Change is partnering with **PCI** (Project Concern International), a large and influential non-profit with over 50 years of experience in administering aid programs globally. Like many of the leading non-profits today — PCI recognizes that one of the fastest ways to bring about lasting change in developing nations is through the financial empowerment of women. This is what inspired them to create the "Women Empowered" program.

The "Women Empowered" program is a comprehensive training process (running 1 - 2 years in length) that helps women in undeveloped communities learn invaluable literacy, financial and leadership skills.

This program teaches women how to work together, pool their resources and income and help each other start and grow small businesses. These small businesses bring in money that these women then use to feed and care for their children, send them to school, and invest in other projects that benefit their communities as a whole.

The results are impressive! In just a few short years, Women Empowered has already helped over 400,000 women in twelve different countries learn key skills and start on the road to financial independence.

The women taking part in the Women Empowered program have collectively saved over 2 million dollars, and launched over 13,000 different micro-businesses in various countries. 98% of the women report less violence at home and 97% feel they now have influence in their communities as a result of taking part in this training.[18]

[2]http://www.insideeldercare.com/uncategorized/more-elderly-parents-living-with-adult-children/

[3, 4]http://cfs-fcee.ca/wp-content/uploads/sites/2/2013/11/Factsheet-2013-11-Student-Debt-EN.pdf

[5]http://ftalphaville.ft.com/2014/06/10/1873182/the-growth-of-us-student-loan-debt-causes-and-consequences/

[6]http://www.theguardian.com/money/2014/jan/21/record-levels-young-adults-living-home-ons

[7]https://en.wikipedia.org/wiki/Student_loans_in_the_United_States

[8]http://www.delawaresleepsociety.org/wp-content/uploads/2015/04/The-Impact-of-Environmental-Toxins-on-Health.pptx

[9]http://www.nrdc.org/health/

[10]http://www.cbc.ca/player/News/TV+Shows/ID/2667577656/

[11]http://www.webmd.com/allergies/tc/environmental-illness-toxins-in-our-environment

[12]http://www.canada.com/vancouversun/news/story.html?id=57586947-9466-4fcf-bb1b-2c464dd19e5c#__federated=1

[13]http://www.cbc.ca/natureofthings/episodes/programmed-to-be-fat

[14]http://isagenixhealth.net/wp-content/uploads/2014/09/Skidmore_Study_Presentation_092614.pdf

[15]http://www.motherearthnews.com/natural-health/nutrition/nutrient-deficiency-zm0z13jjzmat.aspx

[16 http://www.kolaporegardens.com/what-is-c-s-a/

[17]http://www.the6healthyhabits.com/biggest-causes-of-stress-2.html

[18]http://www.womenunitedforchange.com/anke-mayer/

Chapter 2

CAN THESE PROBLEMS BE SOLVED?

Yes, they can be solved. And that's because you are capable of way more than you may want to believe or admit. Each of the problems outlined has a common denominator. Every problem mentioned is a stressor. Stress is inevitable and according to the World Health Organization (WHO), STRESS is the number ONE killer in the world. Learn how to think about stress differently and deal with stress effectively and most of the problems cease to be an issue; they become just another aspect of life. However, given as each of the aforementioned problems seem to require different approaches, I'll spend a chapter on each of the major stressors, giving you a multitude of de-stressing tools for your toolbox, and also teach you something I've already mentioned, the Happiness Cycle.

The Happiness Cycle

Happiness is something we all want to have in our life. Some people just expect they would be happy under certain conditions like having a loving and caring partner in life or having access to unlimited funds so they can do what they like every day.

Others constantly work towards that happy state of mind because what makes them happy today may not make them happy tomorrow. Are we even supposed to be happy on a daily basis? It seems that often in life happiness gets lost along the way. We are too busy, too tired, something unforeseen happens or we blame someone else for our unhappiness. Maybe you feel you missed an opportunity to happiness because you did not do this, that or the other thing and now there seems to be no way to attain it anymore. You missed the boat as they say.

Keep in mind something that makes your friend happy may not be something that makes you happy and vice versa. Different things make different people happy. And some people never feel happy. They always complain and make sarcastic remarks about happiness as if it were something out of a fairy tale that just seems like pure luck and not meant for them anyway. So, what is happiness and how can we make sure we live it almost daily?

I believe that we are all here to do what makes us happy. We all have certain gifts or individual talents that were given to us to be used—to perfect them, have fun with them and make others happy with them.

Now, you may think that sounds like hog-wash. "I do not have time for that. I have to work to earn a living. I have chores and duties waiting for me at home. I do not have time for hobbies!" Relax! Take a deep breath. Let's look at this from a different perspective and you will see what I mean.

Happiness is not something that fits a particular mold. Happiness is a state of mind. It is constantly evolving and will take different shapes as you evolve during your life.

As a child you are happy when you get what you want, feel safe, loved and protected. Wait a minute. That actually never changes when we get older, or does it? Maybe there are just a few things we can add to that basic formula of happiness once we take on responsibility for ourselves and our children and others.

Life is a constant challenge that makes us look for happiness, work at happiness, create our happiness and take responsibility for our own happiness. Because a life without it is just no fun at all, so we better make it happen. Happiness helps us with productivity, creativity, health and income.

Your life includes so many new challenges that once you recognize and acknowledge them, you can manage them better and find ways to overcome, work around or incorporate them in a new and different way. After all challenges are there to teach us, make us stronger and smarter, and help us evolve as a person.

And yes, in all that craziness that we encounter daily it is possible to be happy too!

Think about it. How often have you been afraid of something that never happened? How often have you been worried about a situation that in the end turned out just fine? How often have you wasted time pondering what to do so that you are prepared for the worst? And in the end did the worst ever happen? When you only focus on negative, worrisome fantasies you will feel paralyzed, unable to invite positivity and happiness in your life. We all do have these fearful thoughts from time to time. To some extent it helps us realize that we have to change something in our life to avoid a dreadful situation or find solutions to the problems we are afraid of. It can also help us to realize how strong we actually are.

Being scared of something that is out of your control does not serve you because it may never happen anyway. So why waste your time on such thoughts? Instead trust in your abilities and talents and decide to ask for help when you really need it. When you make that shift and decide to live in the moment, life gets easier.

According to Shawn Achor, an expert on positive psychology, how much money we make, where we live, and our family situation or genes only account for 10% of our happiness. The other 90% comes from how we process information like any news, situations, what we hear and see.

Mr. Achor found out in his research that when we perceive stress as a threat it shuts down our brain and our immune system. On the other hand, a positive brain increases productivity, emotional and material abundance increases, and health outcomes improve.

The old Greeks believed that happiness is the joy you feel moving towards your potential.

There are certain strategies you can apply to respond to life's challenges with your full potential.

- Learn and practice how to respond to stress of all kinds (Chapter 3)
- Practice strategies to let go of fear and anxiety (Chapter 4)
- Learn how to trust yourself and how amazing you are (Chapter 5)
- Discover strategies to be stronger and smarter with age (Chapter 6)
- Learn how not to do it all alone (Chapter 7)
- Learn what you can do not only for yourself but also with ease for others and live a life of purpose (Chapter 8)
- Why I do what I do and how you can help too (Chapter 9)

Let's start by focusing not on what is broken but on what is working, and how to improve from there. One of my favourite reminders is "Life is 10% of what happens to you and 90% of how you respond."

It is important to exercise regularly, to take good care of your body, to have good relationships so that in a social aspect you do not feel alone but grounded and supported. We are a social animal, one who thrives as part of a group or a community.

These things being done, you must learn to trust that whatever challenges come your way you will be able to master them. I will share strategies with you here so that you learn how to calm down, how to de-stress, so you can focus on what's really important at the moment.

And you don't feel discouraged because this, that or the other thing doesn't work so well anymore if, for example, you're getting older. You have unique gifts that, once you embrace them, can change your life and contribute in some way to the life of people you care about, or even society at large.

You will realize also that by finding your life purpose—which is something that excites you, you dream about, gets you out of bed early every day, something you truly enjoy and can't shut up about —there's no need to feel bad or stressed anymore because doing something you are pumped up about shifts your focus, your thoughts and your behavior. When you are excited about something, even as you get older, your limitations no longer matter. You are looking for ways to make up for them in some other ways. You're doing what you love! In my case that's impacting lives by empowering others through my business, with my charity; and that is why I am writing this book. Earlier in my life my family was my focus, supporting my husband in his career and my son through school and his hockey career. While working in my banking career I was helping people to manage their debt or investments. I still volunteer at our primary school in a reading program for grades 1-3 because I love to work with kids. Think about what excites you!

The Happiness Cycle ties it all in

- Are you **taking care of yourself,** your mind, body and soul? Before you can help others you have to help yourself.
- How do you **feel, think, and talk about yourself?**
- How much **confidence and believe do you have in yourself,** your talents and gifts to manage and overcome obstacles and challenges?
- Do you celebrate **your uniqueness,** or do you try to hide it to fit in?
- Does your life **include others**? Are you asking for help when you need it? Are you listening and supportive of others?
- Are you part of a social circle or do you have a group of **friends** to share common interests, have fun with and enjoy? After all, I believe we are all here to enjoy our life.
- **Love** is essential to our happiness. When you love who you are, know that you are loved for who you are, confident in who you are, you cannot help but to pass it on and share your love with others. In love we are created and with love we thrive. Love is all we need, as the Beatles once proclaimed.
- How often are you grateful for your life, the things you have access to, the people in your life who love you, or teach you, for the events in life that make you successful or remind you to improve in some way? **Gratitude** is your key to lasting happiness and sustained success. It completes the Happiness Cycle.
- **When you enjoy life because you are healthy, grateful for what you already have, confident about yourself, have fun in what you do and are able to find meaning in what you do, there are no limits to your success.**

When one piece is missing, lost or broken you can always find a way, create it anew and incorporate it into your personal Happyness Cycle. In fact the other parts of the cycle will help you to do that. Let's take a look at what can help you to create and live in your own Happiness Cycle.

Happiness is the foundation to the good life

Happiness means that you are constantly creating a balance of all things going on in your life. It means that you are content with where things are at now. You know that even if your life is not where you want it to be, you can create your personal Happiness Cycle. Happiness gives you the energy to accomplish all things possible. If you have goals that you set out to achieve, it is happiness and passion that drive you forward to achieve them to make your life better, prompting more happiness.

It is said that "Nothing great can be accomplished without passion." But where does passion come from? How do you get the passion needed to accomplish your goals, leading to more happiness that your good life requires?

You develop passion when you realize what you love to do daily, not because you have to but because you want to. What you are passionate about makes you feel good. It is the thing you are so excited about, that you dream about it, think about it all the time, and you enjoy it so much that it never feels like work. **What are you excited about right now?**

Look at where you're at in life at this very moment. Where are you now? Where were you at one year ago? Has anything changed? You can attain happiness by being grateful every day for the things life has provided you so far.

At this moment, if you aren't happy, think about what needs to change to make you feel happy. What can you change yourself? Where would you need some help? How will any change impact your future? How will you feel once you have achieved it?

Being grateful for everything you already have in your life is different for everyone. I am grateful for my family and friends, the people who love me, my past experiences and even mistakes because they have prepared me for new challenges and goals that lie ahead. I am

> I am grateful for
> 1) My family, the love of my life ♡ and all the children who are part of it.
> 2) My friends old and new, near and far and the love & happiness they create.
> 3) God's guidance and protection at all times.
> 4) The Challenges that come my way to help me grow and overcome limits.
> 5) The opportunities that arise to provide meaning & fulfillment.
> 6) The community I live in that makes me feel I belong.
> 7) Nature's beauty that surrounds me and keeps me grounded.
> 8) The food that nourishes and keeps me healthy.
> 9) The daily tasks that keep me focused.
> 10) The dreams and goals I have. They push me forward each day. ☺

grateful for the air I breathe, the food I have access to, for the natural environment I enjoy at home and while traveling, for my health and abilities… I can go on and on. There is always so much to be grateful for when you take the time to think about it. **What are you grateful for today?** Once you change your perspective, you start your own Happiness Cycle. When you're grateful, your line of thought shifts from negative to positive. It helps you realize how lucky you already are when you acknowledge everything that is already going well for you. It changes your mood, the way you feel, the way you look….you may start to smile more often. The regular practice of gratitude even effects your behaviour, health and any success you are looking for in your life.

As a practicing energy healer I know and work with the power of thought. Negative thinking lowers our vibrational energy. Negative thinking weakens our immune system and create blockages and imbalances in our body, that can lead to many different health problems, chronic and otherwise.

Positive thinking on the other hand raises our vibrational energy. It has a positive effect on the every cell in our body. It makes us radiate and be attractive to others. Positive thinking makes us more beautiful and fun to be around with. It allows us to focus on solutions rather than fear. It is a unique gift we received to overcome challenges, disappointments, sadness, injustice, anger, setbacks and injuries. Gratitude practiced daily will help you to maintain positive thinking to shift the way your life unfolds.

Gratitude over time creates a happier you, who wants to take care of yourself, appreciate yourself, and wants to live a life filled with love.

With a happy mind, you find that you have more energy to get done what actually needs to get done, focus on what really matters and pursue endeavors that give you joy and fulfillment. You will also notice that you are attracting different people and circumstances into your life. Your life will change for the better. Some people call this the Law of Attraction. It is a strategy many successful people are using and have used from Ancient Greek to modern civilization. [19]

Poor self-confidence – acknowledge the problem, change what is not working, recognize your inner gifts and use them!

Do you remember somebody telling you that you were good enough? That you're doing an excellent job? If you can't remember, take a step back. Think about this for a minute.

What is your opinion of yourself? How do you think you're doing? And whose standards do you need to meet?

Chances are that if you are not satisfied with your performance, you may have low self-esteem, a low level of self-confidence or both.

Do you think you're ugly or stupid sometimes? Don't worry, because at some point, everyone else does, too. Do you think everyone else thinks you're ugly and stupid sometimes? Not to fret, because as before, everyone else feels that way too.

Too often, we discredit ourselves. Too often, when we are faced with a lack of validation from others, we form opinions of ourselves that may not be true! We are all beautiful in our unique way, and definitely not dumb! It's our own lack of confidence in ourselves that leave us feeling defeated and in despair. Instead you may want to ask yourself, "What can I do differently the next time to achieve a different result? How can I improve **so I feel better about myself**?"

Do you have a talent or a hobby that you can contribute? Do you find that people ask you for help or advice?

The thought-trap that is low self-esteem can be solved by realizing that you do matter, that your gifts contribute to help others. There are about 7 billion people on this earth, and the beauty of it is that no two persons are exactly alike. If you want to achieve a result of significance you will be best of by leveraging your unique skills with those of others.

So take some time to think about what gifts you bring to the table, because I guarantee that you have something the next-door neighbours don't have.

What is it that comes easily to you? What do you enjoy doing? What gives you a thrill when you do it even though you are not totally sure that you can do it? What can you get excited about? By identifying your strengths, you will soon discover your uniqueness, increase your sel-esteem and become more confident in what you do and who you are.

Balance, stress, anxiety, no time – meditation, prioritize and schedule your time

In this day and age, it's hard to keep up with everything. Some of you may be in school, work, and have a family to take care of. Such is life. Everything seems to be top priority, so it's important to keep up with all areas in your life so as not to lose everything, including our minds.

Sometimes, however, it can be a little much. We pile expectations on us and we feel we have to meet them; we just have to go with them in order to stay on top. Have you ever felt that you are in control of your life only to realize that stuff happens? Now you need to go with the new paradigm, circumstance or shift. As much as you want to be in control, life requires you to remain flexible. Outwardly, you might appear okay, yet inwardly, you may feel as though you want to give up.

The natural reaction when stress begins to grow to an overwhelming degree is that we automatically want to continue as we had planned, using ways we have used in the past. What I found is that most of the time we create our own stress. It is hard to change the way you approach obstacles or changes, yet they may appear in your life to change YOU.

It helps to take a step back and take a breath. To meditate for a few minutes every day is a very healthy thing to do. Meditation helps to reset your emotions, calm you down and when practiced regularly aligns your behaviours and thoughts with your inner spirit. While meditating you may notice that your previous actions may not have been the best way to go about a situation. Aligning your body, mind and soul is a great way to recognize and establish new ways of thinking and practice new behaviour that will serve you better going forward. There are many different ways to meditate, from yoga classes to guided tapping, see http://www.tapping.com.

You have to find the one that works best for you. For those of you who are constantly pressed for time I recommend as a starting point https://www.zen12.com/about.

Another equally important way to manage your stress is by using a day planner or calendar to schedule the things that are important in your life. Although timelines may change or shift organizing your day is a great way to ensure you are not forgetting important meetings, events or timelines and to account for "me time" and "family time." It helps you to stay on top of things that are important to you without getting overwhelmed!

However, allowing stress to get the better of you has deadly consequences. Stress drives up cortisol levels, causing you to store fat, which puts you at risk for developing a whole host of health problems linked to obesity, including but not limited to: diabetes, heart disease, and several cancers.

With that being said, I highly recommend that you take at least a few minutes out of the daily grind and just pay attention to you. Schedule some "me" time in your calendar at least once a week and check in with yourself and your current needs. It can be at any time of the day; basically whenever you aren't busy. I like to take time at the end of the night and meditate for 10-15 minutes. Or instead of watching TV I get comfortable on my couch and reflect on the day's events, and make sense of them and my emotions toward them. This way, the time I spend by myself allows me to prepare for the next day's excursions.

The time you spend by yourself can be spent however you feel necessary. If you don't have any idea how to relax, start a new hobby, or join a group of like-minded positive people who share your values and interests. These examples are constructive, produce results, and are both mentally healthy ways to de-stress.

Job security – always make sure you take advantage of opportunities (Keep learning, remain open to new ways of thinking and doing)

In today's economy, employers are highly selective of who gets to fill that position. You need to be at your best and willing to do more.

In turn, this scenario forces turnover rates to rise, as employers constantly try to find someone better who has all the skills and training to get the job done right and in less time for less compensation. So, how do you stay up-to-date with the needs of the job market? You don't want to be overlooked for a promotion because your skills aren't in line with the ever-changing requirements of your career.

Update your resumé. It's perfectly acceptable to take classes that pertain to your job. If you love your job, find a few at the local college. Talk to your employer and find out what skills they are looking for and are willing to pay for. Make it part of your review or evaluation process to avoid any misunderstanding and map out your career plan.

If you currently are unemployed and look for a job, the unemployment office might be offering vocational classes that you can take. A key tip is to educate yourself, and grow your mind because knowledge is power!

Working in a job can be limiting you in your abilities. You will only get paid what your employers wants to pay for your work and you will never have job security in our current economy anymore. More and more companies prefer to hire independent contractors instead, to keep costs low. They do not have to pay employment insurance, health insurance or invest in training. It appears to me that the future belongs to the Evolved Economy, where you decide what you want to do, with who you want to work, how many hours you want to put in and how much time you will dedicate to upgrade your skills. In essence your abilities and effort will ultimately determine how successful you will become, and how much money you will earn.

Not everyone is ready to take such steps. You have to decide your course of action. Just remember that what seems hard in the beginning will be rewarding down the road. Those of you who have a driver's license can attest to that!

Low energy/lack of spirit – identify and do things that increase your spirit and state of happiness

Unhappiness is draining—physically and mentally. If you suffer from depression, you may feel like you never want to leave the bed ever again, because the drive to get up and take care of business just isn't there.

Even if you don't have depression, we all have had those times where we just don't have the spirit and the heart to want to carry on. This is a very dangerous and self-destructive state of mind, because it is during times like these that we risk derailing our progress in light of the happiness we've felt in the past, which just *pushed* us to achieve the tasks needed.

And this goes hand in hand with feeling burnt out. Too much stress does that. Occasionally, if no preventive measures are taken to try and reduce the stress we have in our lives, we become overwhelmed and dis-spirited. We start to not want to pursue the goals that are supposed to improve our lives, because we get disillusioned into not caring.

And again, this comes back to finding your purpose in life. We are not here to be sad and depressed forever. We are here to do something meaningful, use our body and our abilities effectively to achieve, create value, serve others and first of all enjoy life along the way. Remind yourself of everything you have access to right now like fresh air to breathe, sunshine to enjoy, water to drink, access to nature and its beauty to rejuvenate, family and/or friends for love and support, your unique qualities others envy and admire, a home for shelter, knowledge and experience you acquired to make better choices in the future. Maybe you are blessed with good looks, a healthy body or a sharp mind. When you think about it seriously there are many things, people or circumstances you can be grateful for.

Using some of that "me" time to practise that hobby may sound counter-productive, yet is shown to reset your mental gears, so you end up coming back refreshed and ready to tackle your projects once again and yield much better, greater results!

Other important ways to stay and keep happy are things we seem to take for granted. A walk in nature can help you rebalance your mood. You may also never have thought about a core part in creating and maintaining a healthy mind (and body). It is the food you eat that fuels **and** balances the energy that keeps you going.

The food you eat has an effect on how you think, feel and function. I will talk about that in more detail in Chapters 3 and 4.

Financial stress, job security – don't be afraid of losing your job. Be open to what your spirit is telling you. You can always find a way forward.

Going back to the topic of job security, it is common in this economy to be fearful of losing your job. Layoffs have been imminent in any financial crisis; almost every government shutdown has witnessed quite a number people being without a job due to downsizing, less demand in certain services or shifts in technology. This is a normal part of how the economy works; there are always economic booms and busts. However, there has never been a shortage of jobs, because you can always find one in at least some part of the country.

Most of us look at the situation this way:
- People lose their job, because their skills are no longer required.
- People did not perform at the standards the employer thought they should.
- The employer could replace them with someone else at a lower cost.
- The company dissolved or went through restructuring.

Now think about your situation this way:
- I lost my job because I am supposed to do something different.
- I lost my job because I am better at something else.
- I lost my job because I have to take better care of myself first.
- I can be more successful in a different career.

If you are reading this and have recently become down on your luck, then bear in mind that it happenes to everyone at some point in their lives. Almost everyone has experienced financial insecurity as a result of the job economy. Understanding this, there are multiple resources that you can utilise until you once again land on solid, stable ground, and know that the Universe wants you to change something in yourself that you would never do if you were comfortable with your life. Being in a tight spot helps you finding ways to overcome and change your current situation. Be patient with yourself, ask for help and advice, use the support others offer for the interim and work on yourself to create lasting change for yourself. If you are in this situation, do know that it's only temporary, and this too shall pass. Remain open to new and even different ideas and have courage to try those you feel good about.

There are counsellors that will help you realise and identify your true gifts and inclinations to point you to a new career. If you do decide to pursue a new profession, let your spirit be your guide. Be open to what you truly want to do, even if it may be lower-paying. Because as the old adage goes, "Choose a job you like and you'll never have to work a day in your life." The objective is to aim for more happiness in what you do and the money will follow. When you enjoy what you do, you will always deliver good quality and service. People value that and will pay you accordingly. Consider that happiness will guide you to what you do best so you can enjoy the life you deserve.

Environmental stress

Have you ever wondered how the weather could have an effect on your mood? When it gets colder and the nights grow longer, have you ever noticed that the early sunsets may affect your mood?

These questions all tie into how environmental stress shapes our behaviour. Environmental stress is defined as any outside factors, like crowds, noise, weather, pollution and heat, that contribute to how we act. Whether you like it or not, the elements all have a say in whether or not we develop health problems. This is different from any day-to-day stress that we experience. Environmental stress is an external influence that has an effect on our body and mind.

During the winter months, many people develop seasonal affective disorder (SAD). The lack of sunlight not only changes our circadian rhythm during the winter months, it "also regulates the daily timing of more than a hundred functions that we know, and probably a thousand that we don't, including the manufacture of our hormones."* Sound Sleep by Michael Colgan PhD.

It is estimated that more than 20% of the North American population suffer from SAD, which differs from depression in that it will subside once the daily sunlight increases.

To fend off depression and build a stronger immune system you also need to supplement with vitamin D3. Because this is a fat soluable vitamin take it with food.

Sunlight aids in the production of vitamin D. With a decrease in sunlight over the winter months your body produces less of that vitamin. So far there have been over 33,000 medical papers published showing evidence that vitamin D plays an important role not only in your physical but also your mental health. According to Dr. Mercola, vitamin D3 does not only show a tremendous protective effect against a variety of different cancers but was also found to reduce depression.[20]

Natural sunlight works wonders for our bodies. The sunlight regulates our "Happiness Hormone", serotonin. So, get out of the house, especially during the winter, to increase your serotonin level and decease your melatonin production! The hormone melanonin increases when it gets dark and is supposed to help us sleep. When you feel sluggish and tired during the day it may be due to an increase in melatonin as well.

Detox regulary through nutritionally supported intermittent fasting to optimize your body's function. Environmental toxins impact our hormone glands, stress our vital organs, and compromise our immune function.

Bottom line

- Get out and into the sunlight as much as possible especially during the winter.
- Supplement with vitamin D3.
- Incorporate intermittent fasting into your lifestyle.

We weren't meant to stay indoors in front of a computer screen or the TV for extended amounts of time; the time we spend outside allows us to get some fresh air and natural sunlight. Without it, we may feel sluggish and depressed. During the months with little sunlight, it is a natural response for people to develop SAD.

Environmental stress can also be attributed to the quality of the atmosphere. If you live in an area with low air quality, you may find yourself getting sick and plagued with respiratory problems, which I don't doubt for a second could add more tension to your life. Areas with high smog are generally more populated; if you live in the heart of the city, then you are at a greater risk for experiencing environmental stress. I will discuss other solutions to address and cope with stress in the next chapter.

However, no matter where you live, there is a way to reduce the amount of stress caused by the environment in which you live. If your lifestyle does not allow for much natural sunlight, then consider getting a sun-lamp. These specialised lamps emulate sunlight, and are far less harsh than fluorescent lights. Use this lamp for 10 minutes at the start of the day for a jump-start on your daily routine, and you'll notice that you have more energy to tackle the day! At day's end, turn the lamp on again for 10 minutes while unwinding.

Try not to do anything else; just focus on soft rays of light that the lamp is radiating, and you will drift off to sleep quickly.[21]

GMOs

Genetically modified organisms (GMOs) are not easy to identify. Monsanto itself, one of the world's largest producers of genetically engineered seeds, defines genetic engineering as altering the genes of plants or animals to exhibit traits that are not naturally theirs. There are no labeling requirements in the US or Canada. In Europe it is mandatory though. In fact there is a law in front of the Senate in the US to pre-empt any future labeling laws. (the DART act was signed this summer by President Obama.)

GMOs are an ingredient in many prepared meals and ready-to-eat food and baked goods. There are basically two main types of GMO seeds, those that are resistent to Roundup (Roundup ready) and those that include the active ingredient of Roundup called glyphosate. In each case the gene in the seed has been altered by replacing a part of it with the strain of the pesticide. So genetically modified organisms have not been created by growers or farmers in conventional ways but by chemical companies like Monsanto, Dow Chemical, and Dupont, among several others. The amount of pesticide has thereby increased significantly in the food we find in our grocery aisles. Crops mostly affected are corn, soy, potatoes and grain. Your only way to avoid GMOs is by buying organic or GMO-free food. You might still ingest them when you eat out though.

Next-generation GMOs are designed to be resistant to combinations of herbicides. Enlist Duo, which was recently green-lighted, is resistant to both glyphosate and 2,4-D, a major ingredient in Agent Orange.

I take the position that GMOs are not ethical in food production, because they can not only be harmful to your health but also harm the economy of farming careers. This advance in science has also been shown to produce long-term effects on the human body, and even develop cancer. The pesticides left behind in these plants and animals can be found in the bloodstream. It is simply unhealthy to deposit these poisons in your body.

GMOs are also harmful to the environment, because genetically-modified crops are less sustainable than regular, untreated crops. Now the herbicides, pesticides and fungicides to grow these crops increasingly show up in the watertables around those fields and in our water supply.

Next time you're out shopping, look for organic foods that have not been genetically-modified. The farmer's market is an excellent way to purchase homegrown selections, and all the while buying from local farmers and supporting small businesses; or opt for your local CSA program.[22][23][24][25]

Relationships, no love

Relationships can fit into many forms. They are not just confined to romantic relationships. We have relationships with everyone, because all a relationship really is, is just a description of how we interact with others.

You have a relationship with your neighbours. You have a relationship with your co-workers. You have a relationship with friends and relatives. All of the people in your life have an impact on how you feel, how you react, and the choices you make along the way. On the other hand, you also impact their life. Without them, your life would probably be different. Simply put, a relationship is really just a reliance on one another; a describer of the footprint they have left on your life.

Love is the same way. Showing people you care comes in many different forms. It could be telling your child to be careful when crossing the road. It could be buying your co-workers a round of coffee. It could be a kiss on the cheek from your significant other. Simply stated, there are an endless variety of ways through which love is expressed.

The need to be loved is an essence of being human. Instinctively, we all want to feel as though we belong to something greater than ourselves. A sense of belonging, and a sense of being accepted for who we are is a basic need; without it, we may feel neglected, which can be a justification for developing depression and suicidal thoughts. The feeling of not being loved can also block us from living life to our full potential because we do not have the confidence to live out loud, trusting in our abilities and gifts.

In this life, we are never truly alone. We all depend on one another for support, encouragement, and love. We cannot exist without one another. Somebody depends on you, and you depend on somebody. You are needed, and valued for what you can give to others, even if you feel as if you have nobody to turn to. I can guarantee that somebody is out there who wants to hear from you.

How cool is it that the same God who created mountains, rivers, oceans and galaxies looked at you and thought the world needed one of you too? Ever thought of yourself this way? Who would contribute your specific talents and ideas to the world? It doesn't matter if you are single, have children, parents or are in a romantic relationship; someone who relies on you counts on your effort, your talents, and your love because of your unique relationship with them.

If you feel that nobody cares about you, then I guarantee that among the 7 billion inhabitants of the earth, at least one person does. Make sure you let them know how much you care, are willing to support them or their causes; lend your ear to listen to their problems and help them out as best as you can. Reach out to others, and you will feel their love pouring into you.

No sense of purpose

As we get older and experience life with its ups and downs, we may wonder, "What's the point?" and "Why" are we even here?

Well, we all know that the normal process of life is to be born, grow older, and then we die. Some faiths believe in moving to the afterlife after death, while other belief systems don't. I believe we are all here to grow our minds, our consciousness, our abilities and have a lot of fun along the way.

Sometimes, you might think that every day is alike, where you wake up, carry out your daily routine, and then fall asleep at day's end just to do it all over again. And this process happens over and over again for months and even years on end, without a change to it all. Consequently, you feel bored and unsatisfied with your life, as if the commute to your job is merely a rat race to the grave. I believe life is a gift that we should not waste. When we see each day as an opportunity to learn something new, to meet a fascinating new person, to help someone else during a difficult time, to pass on our own knowledge and wisdom to someone else so their life becomes easier, or by adding a sparkle of fun and love to another life, when we pursue something we truly enjoy each day, then our days will run very fast, become more meaningful, and be more enjoyable.

So ask yourself, what do you enjoy, what can you contribute, what would you love to learn, how can you benefit someone else?

The options are limitless. My parents used to say where there is a will there is a way! It may not be an obvious way but one that is uniquely yours. If you want to be an astronaut, then what is stopping you? Chris Hadfield, a Canadian space commander, dreamed of becoming an astronaut as a little boy at a time when there was no career path to get there. Canada did not have a space program and the Americans preferred US pilots in their program. So Chris pursued a career as a jet pilot because he also loved flying. He did everything he could to be the best among his colleagues. When the opportunity presented itself to get a foot into a career with NASA he worked harder, contributed more than others deemed necessary, got up earlier and hand-delivered his application. Chris Hadfield became the first Canadian Commander of the International Space Station in 2013. Who would have thought? Was it easy? Hell no! Was it achievable? Absolutely, when he knew what he wanted and pursued it with all his might and without any excuses. He had many obstacles to overcome yet Chris did not get deterred.

If you want to go on a vacation destination you always dream about, put it on your vision board. Put that board in a dominant place in your home to keep it in the forefront of your thoughts. Put it on your screen saver on your computer, so it pops up first thing when you start your computer. Think about a way to put some money aside every month towards your vacation fund. Talk to others about your plans. Think about it when you go to bed and when you wake up in the morning.

I hope you see the pattern. If something is truly important to you, whatever it may be, you can make it happen. It is something to look forward to every day. It is then that you will find a way to bring it into your life.

Your purpose in life may not be the vacation destination or a career but it is the tangible aspect that drives you to pursue it. It may be that through your actions you inspire others, you advance science, or bring joy into not just your life but maybe someone else's too.

What you were meant to do in this life is certain to come to you at some point, but you have to take the first steps in looking for what excites you, drives you; remain relentless in pursuing your joy in life and your purpose will reveal itself.

No participation

Continuing on discussing the human need to belong, there are many benefits to participating in a group. It gives you the opportunity to meet new people and connect with others who have similar interests. Interacting with like-minded people is good for you; it expands your mind, nourishes your spirit, creates opportunities to make new friends, learn new ideas and concepts and make you feel comfortable. Or it can even create a sense of belonging to something larger than yourself. In any case you will notice what a value you can be in someone else's life.

Try putting in some volunteer work. There is an endless array of groups that want to work towards a better cause and may look for your specific talents. Look into working at a food bank or an animal shelter. If you want to help out, look for a charity that matches your interests. This way, volunteer work will be fun and rewarding, on both ends. Participating in activities such as these will not only help those in need, but it also gives you a great sense of accomplishment. So volunteer, and your participation will reward you with a sense of contribution and appreciation.

Health

The way you feel is directly correlated to your health. Your health is not just the current state of your physical body. If your mind and your spirit are not in a healthy state you will literally feel it physically. The same is true the other way around. If the body hurts, we will not feel as happy.

Physical illness is often a manifestation of a body that is not at ease, not aligned with the mind and the spirit, hence *disease*. In modern medicine we usually receive treatment for physical symptoms, and not very often for the underlying causes to our condition.

To live a truly happy and fulfilling life on purpose, our own health is the foundation that helps us achieve everything else. If the body is not well, nothing else really matters. In that sense I believe that our health is our true wealth. It is essential to keep our body in good shape and feed our mind with happy meaningful thoughts that are in line with our spirit's purpose.

How do we do that?

Feed your body good nutritious food, move it often in ways that you enjoy, like dancing, Yoga, running, team sports etc. Incorporate meditation into your daily life to connect with your spirit, surround yourself with positive like-minded people, feed your mind meaningful information that helps it grow and expand in a positive loving way. And have a lot of fun!

Underlying causes to physical illness or pain can also be caused by blockages in our meridians, the highways of our energy that run through our body like our blood vessels or nerves. Blockages can appear in any part of the body and are very often created though our mind. They may appear after traumatic experiences like injuries or accidents. Very often they are created through negative thoughts like anxiety, fear, disappointment, anger at ourselves or others in our immediate surrounding. Energy healers, acupuncturists and other naturopathic practitioners can help to break up those blockages so that the body can heal.

The point is to always treat your mind and spirit as you would your physical body.

Spirituality – care for your mind, body and spirit

Spirituality is the awareness and celebration that we all are part of a higher power. No matter your religion, most of us know that there is something outside our control that helps us on our life path.

Being spiritually aware is a wonderful way to get in touch with your inner self and connect with that higher power. Some call that power God, some refer to several Gods, others call it the Universe. Your individual religion is your way to experience, love and celebrate that higher power. It is often part of your heritage. No matter the religion, they all need to be respected as something divine and holy. Every belief is mostly tied to specific customs we feel familiar with. They help us to understand something that we cannot see nor touch. All religions have one original belief in common; that there is a higher power that looks after us, loves us and takes care of us. This sense in its true form is meant to help us to trust, release our fear, take care of each other, and respect one another.

We are all part of something truly amazing. This higher power is creating new life all the time. We usually call it nature because it is so normal to us. Yet quite often we may forget that we are all connected somehow. If our environment is in trouble, our health suffers. Sometimes species disappear and we do not always understand how that is impacting us in some way too. Most often we believe that we know everything, only to learn later that God or the Universe actually thought of everything already in a much broader way we cannot always comprehend. That is what spirituality means to me. It respects all religious beliefs.

When you appreciate and care for the body that envelops your spirit and mind, believe and trust in a higher power of love and respect, and help your mind to let go of negative thoughts, then you will find peace and happiness to live your life to the fullest.

Yoga is one method that helps your body stay strong, release any tension, connect your mind and spirit to create balance between these three. It is a complex set of moves that help you stay flexible, strong, and focused. It is a form of meditation that connects body, mind and soul, as it has been practiced for thousands of years. It relaxes, strengthens, and balances body, mind and soul.

With all of this being said, the complex human body is a culmination of the body, mind, and spirit and the environment we live in. All parts work together to make you who you are. You cannot afford to tend to one aspect while neglecting the others. It is important to apply self-care to the body, mind, and spirit and our environment in order to feel happy and live a healthy life.

[19]https://en.m.wikipedia.org/wiki/Esther_Hicks

[20]http://articles.mercola.com/sites/articles/archive/2014/01/02/vitamin-d-deficiency-depression.aspx

[21]http://www.stresstips.com/the-role-of-environmental-stress-in-your-mood

[22]http://www.nongmoproject.org/learn-more/

[23]http://www.ewg.org/issue/genetically-engineered-food/ge-foods-not-natural

[24]https://www.google.com/url?q=http://articles.mercola.com/sites/articles/archive/2015/08/04/hr-1599-bans-gmo-labeling-laws.aspx&sa=U&ved=0ahUKEwjXnoPnw_3JAhXkjYMKHbOLAL4QFggQMAQ&client=internal-uds-cse&usg=AFQjCNEul6vBsW65qtg2KMc-P_8ak3pWHg

[25]http://articles.mercola.com/sites/articles/archive/2015/09/01/gmos-herbicides-public-health.aspx

Chapter 3

RELIEVING STRESS

I like to manage stress by going to its core and then finding specific solutions for whatever stressor is affecting me at the moment. Adaptogens play a big part in how I deal with STRESS: (source - Isagenix). They work like a "stress vaccine" for your brain.

How we react to mental stress is controlled by a complex interaction between the hypothalamus, pituitary gland and adrenal glands. These three structures form the hypothalamus-pituitary-adrenal (HPA) axis and help control mood, energy levels, body temperature, and immunity.

The hypothalamus secretes hormones that act on the pituitary gland that can cause or stop the release of pituitary hormones. The adrenal glands release stress hormones like cortisol and adrenaline. The role of the HPA axis is expansive, yet its primary function relates to how we respond to stress. In the first stage of the stress response the hypothalamus releases a hormone that signals the pituitary to "activate" the adrenal gland to release cortisol. Cortisol is a classical stress hormone that is increased during times of stress.

Cortisol release is a normal and healthy response to normal levels of stress. This is certainly true for acute stress. However, chronic exposure to stress, like job pressures or family demands, can add on heavy doses of mental stress. Chronic stress seems to be a hallmark of modern life and can cause dysfunction in both the HPA axis and cortisol secretion patterns. A prolonged stress response can negatively affect one of the most important organs in your body; your brain. As a result, you may experience decreased cognition, anxiety and poor mental performance.

However, bioactive substances from adaptogens can help by functioning like "stress vaccines," by reducing the over-exaggerated response to a stressor and by helping maintain healthy levels of cortisol. This effect has been noted in a randomized double-blind, placebo-controlled study using ashwagandha (Withania somnifera) supplements in adults experiencing high levels of stress. Not only did researchers find decreased levels of perceived stress in subjects taking ashwagandha, but cortisol was also decreased. The researchers suggested that the supplement's "therapeutic activity may be attributed, at least in part, to its effect on the hypothalamic-pituitary-adrenal axis, which regulates serum cortisol concentration."

The idea of a "stress vaccine" was coined by adaptogen expert Alexander Panossian, who explained that adaptogens mimic stress itself and create an adaptive response to stress. This translates into increasing the work capacity of the brain by being "stress-protective" or "restorative." Dr. Panossian reasons that the chemical structures of adaptogens are similar to hormones like adrenaline. Components of the herbs may also resemble corticosteroids, which help to inactivate a stress response.

Adaptogens, being restorative or stress-protective, improve attention and focus while reducing risk of mental fatigue. In this regard, adaptogens are markedly different from stimulants. Adaptogenic effects have been noted to occur after only one single dose. In this double-blinded, placebo-controlled, randomized study investigators used a single dose of a combination of rhodiola (Rhodiola rosea), schisandra (Schisandra chinensis) and eleuthero (Eleutherococcus senticosus). Mental performance, such as attention, speed and accuracy, was assessed in tired individuals performing stressful cognitive tasks. The subjects in the adaptogen group exhibited improved attention and increased speed and accuracy during stressful cognitive tasks. There was also a tendency to reduce the percentage of errors, which meant better accuracy, quality of the work, and degree of care.

Other plants like wolfberry (Lycium barbarum) and bacopa (Bacopa monnieri) also increase resistance to psychological stress by acting as powerful antioxidants to support brain health. This is particularly true for older individuals where decreased mental performance is more apparent. For example, in a study investigating the effects of bacopa in memory improvement in older people over a 12-week period, bacopa significantly improved memory acquisition and retention.

Unfortunately, in today's modern lifestyles, too many people are succumbing to chronic stress—with poor health outcomes as a result. While exercise and good nutrition is always advised, adaptogens help your body to combat stress, focus your mind and elevate your daily performance. They are natural botanicals that strengthen the body's capacity to resist and reduce stress as well as promote physical and mental performance. Truly something that we all could use. Because adaptogenic herbs have the ability to balance your cortisol levels, they also play an important role in healthy sustainable weight loss.[26]

Environmental stress: toxicity, noise and radiation

We cannot always avoid stress but we can implement strategies. Adaptogens don't just work on your brain but they also affect the way your body deals with stress. Additionally, there are many other methods that can be used, like time management, goal setting, practicing mindfulness and meditation and the use of delegation. Let's study some of these.

There's no "me" time

A moral system exists that admonishes its members to take the 24 inch ruler and apportion it to the 24 hours in a day. Eight hours for work, eight hours for sleep and eight hours for family, prayer and leisure. This system is very old, yet it still recognizes the need for there to be reasonable "down time" in this life.

Eight hours is a lot of time, but what do we do with it? We rush through the day like frightened rabbits, racing off in all directions, thinking that we must pack everything we've got into those poor eight hours.

Well, time may be fleeting, but there's hardly cause for worry, fear or any other form of stress. A small package of instruments can virtually eliminate "bad stress" from your life. I say bad stress because some forms of stress are actually good for you; they give you an edge when you really need it. The rest of the time? Stress just burns up your energy and your day.

The way to make certain there's enough me time for you in a day is to schedule important priorities for you in your scheduler first, like your workouts, hairdresser, reading or fun time with family and friends. Prioritize the list so that at the beginning of each day you begin with the most important task (to you), continuing with the next task or activity only when the first one is done. Giving no thought to anything but the current task at hand you will create focus and thus be more effective. You'll pack so much more fun and energy and personal highlights into your day, you'll be amazed.

A note about prioritizing: Make sure that family and work comes first, then schedule time for yourself, whether that is mental, physical or spiritual time. You are still the one making the choices, and this tool can't help you there.

Financial stress and lack of job security

Once one recognizes and accepts that there is no such thing as job security, it becomes a non-issue.

You either deal with it, doing what you can to make yourself as indispensable as possible, going into business for yourself or just treating it as another aspect of life, something that is largely out of your control.

As for the solution to financial stress? It's called budgeting and we cover it next …

Lack of money

Money is the thing people stress most about. So … the way to beat stress about money is to create a budget and stick to it. This includes paying yourself first. From every paycheck you need to take 10% of your earnings for an emergency/opportunity fund. Make sure you don't just put it in your savings account. There are some great money funds out there that will pay decent interest and still allow access to the fund. Talk to your financial advisor—and remember that this is not money for playing with riskier mutual funds. Make an initial budget. See what the numbers say, and then create a new, revised budget you can live with, stress-free!

Monthly Expenses

Housing Expenses:	**Initial**	**Revised**
First Mortgage		
Second Mortgage		
Property Taxes		
House Insurance		
Rent / Condo Fees		
Telephone		
Cell phone		
TV cable		
Internet		
Hydro		
Water / Sewer		
Gas/oil/wood/electric		
Maintenance Contracts		
Other		
Sub Total		
Total Forward:		

Work Expenses:	**Initial**	**Revised**
Transit		
Lunches / Breaks		
Daycare		
Special Clothing		
Sub Total		
Total Forward:		

Living Expenses: **Initial**   **Revised**
Food
Personal Travel
Clothing
Alimony & Support
Auto License
Auto Maintenance
Insurance – Auto
Insurance – Life
Medical/Doctor
Prescription Drugs
Dental
Laundry/Dry Cleaning
Pets
Sub Total
Total Forward:

Personal Expenses: **Initial**   **Revised**
Beverages
Recreation
Babysitter
Personal Grooming
Barber/Hairdresser
Magazines/Newspapers
Gifts
Religious Donations
School Expenses
Donations
Allowances

Invest (10%)
It's really important to pay yourself first.
Debt Payments
These debts shouldn't be more than 30% of your earnings.
Sub Total

Bank loans, credit cards, etc.
Total Forward:
Total

Funds Available: **Initial**   **Revised**
Net Income
Less Total Expenses
Funds Available

The $25,000 idea

There's a story I've heard, although I can't remember the source. It's supposed to be a true story that goes like this...

Back in the days of the great steel companies, a young man came into the office of an executive of a large corporation. He offered to give the executive a single idea that would prove invaluable to him in business. When asked what this idea would cost, the young man replied "Nothing. You take the idea, and try it out for as long as you like. When you're convinced it's the incredible tool I say it is, just send me a cheque for whatever amount you feel it is worth to you." A few months later the young man received a cheque for $25,000.

I don't care if this story is myth or fact. The idea mentioned works.

The idea:

- Draw up a list of the tasks you feel should be done tomorrow.
- When you've completed the list, rearrange those tasks in order of importance, number one being the top priority and the last item on the list being the lowest priority.
- Do those things you dread the most first so they are no longer holding you back.
- Take the first item on the list, and devote all your attention to it until the task is completed.
- When the first task on your list has been completed, move on to the second item, and so on.

- Give absolutely no thought to any items on your list until all preceding items have been completed.

Try this remarkable idea. I'm convinced you won't achieve better results using any other method. Besides, what have you got to lose? Note: I use the method for both business and personal goals.

Construct your prioritized list for tomorrow:
_____
_____
_____
_____
_____
_____

The importance of freeing up time

The sooner you realize there is no such thing as job security and find yourself something you can always fall back on, the happier you'll be. You can try to make yourself indispensable, but unless you are the owner of your own business, free and clear, you aren't ever going to be that person. As for what to fall back on? It's the old saying: do what you love and love what you do. That's where you should be anyway. Who wants to use up a full third of their life doing something they hate to do?

If you still hold a job you dread start your new endeavor in the pockets of your life and remind yourself daily WHY this is important to you. Imagine how different your life will be once you no longer depend on a job you do not enjoy, or even hate.

When thinking about your life, consider it a special gift—today is a gift! That is why it is called the present. To not waste it and make the most use of it, it makes sense to fill your days with something that you enjoy, you love, and schedule everything that needs to be done around that.

Scheduling your day and prioritizing your activities and focus will help you tremendously.

Some people use an old-fashioned desk organizer. I use the calendar on my iPad, which is synchronized with my iPhone and my computer. So no matter when I look at it and no matter what device I use, I know exactly what to do next, and when to do it. This is especially helpful, when you have a full-time job, run a business or have a young family. Scheduling your day ensures that there is still YOU time, that you are not missing any important events or appointments, and that the things you love have priority. It puts you in control of your day. It helps you manage your day, so you are less likely to become overwhelmed. It provides focus, so you do everything more efficiently, more diligently, and with more enjoyment.

If you have never used this technique, you may have to practice. Here are a few helpful tips: First put everything in your calendar that you have to do, like your hours at work, certain chores that are inevitable, like preparing meals, picking up the kids from school or daycare, your dentist, etc. Next, put in your calendar all the things that are important to the people you love, like date night with your partner, meeting friends for coffee, calling them on their birthday, volunteer work you signed up for, etc.

Then schedule in everything that is important just for you! Time for your hobbies, fitness or workout time, meditation and gratitude time. Some people tell me that now they no longer have time to watch TV. In the end you decide what is important in your life, and you will have to prioritize!

Other ways to de-stress ...

Shawn Achor once did an experiment with Google. Over a period of one month, developers in one department had to switch off all their devices, including the computer they were working on. Then for two minutes every day they had to listen to their breath coming into their body and going out. That simple technique of reducing multi-tasking to just focusing on one single task for two minutes each day improved accuracy instantly by 10%, error levels dropped, happiness improved and productivity increased.

Here is another way to destress and improve your feeling of happiness. This may also work for people who are usually very pessimistic. It is a simple two minute daily exercise that can multiply your level of happiness. For the next 30 days write down three new things every day that you are grateful for. This can be something that you recognize needs improvement in your life, or something positive that happened. It can be something very basic like the fact you have a roof over your head and shelter from the elements, having access to food and water, having a person in your life that loves you or needs you, the fact that you have all your senses, vision, smell, hearing and touch, that you are healthy, something you enjoyed today and so forth. It has to be something different every day! By doing this exercise over 30 days you train your brain to be more optimistic. Your brain will then prefer to recognize and notice positives in your life. This will be so significant that, no matter what your genetic setpoints or the environmental impact are, your thoughts will be more positive and ultimately create meaning in your life. Remember "What you focus on grows. What you focus on you will become real, and what you focus on you will become."

You may also try this technique if you tend to be affected by depression. Every day for at least 6 weeks, write down one positive experience you had that day. Be specific and add detail to it like what the weather was that day, what you were wearing, what you said, how you felt, where you were at the time and what the surroundings looked like. Write it all down, adding as much detail as possible. Then throw it out! This exercise creates what Shawn Achor calls a double effect of experience in your brain. According to his research, people would experience a 50% drop in medication for chronic pain. This exercise would create positive thinking and a stamp in the brain, marking that experience as meaningful and positive.

Regular exercise, even a 20 minutes walk in the sunshine, can help you to reduce stress just by being in nature. It also builds up vitamin D naturally. According to Dr. Mercola, previous research has shown having a vitamin D level below 20 ng/mL may raise your risk for depression by as much as 85 percent, compared to having a vitamin D level greater than 30 ng/mL. A number of studies have also confirmed that vitamin D supplementation can help alleviate symptoms of depression.

Most recently, a study published in *Psychiatry Research* looked at healthy women aged 18 to 25 who lived in the Pacific Northwest during the fall, winter and spring, and found that vitamin D insufficiency (30 ng/ml or lower) could predict the emergence of clinically significant depressive symptoms after controlling for factors such as season, body mass index, race, diet, exercise and time spent outdoors.

By the fourth and final week of the study, 46 percent of the women were found to have insufficient levels of vitamin D, and during the course of the study up to 42 percent of them showed signs of clinically significant depression, based on the Center for Epidemiologic Studies depression scale. As reported by HCP Live: vitamin deficiency seems to be widespread and is not always recognized. I found that daily supplementation will help greatly, not only to improve your mood. Researchers have discovered that vitamin D is involved in the biochemical cellular machinery of ALL cells and tissues in your body. Hence, when you don't have enough, your entire body struggles to function optimally. [27][28]

Another common way to de-stress is having a cup of herbal tea. There are many varieties out there meant just for this very thing. Chamomile is one of them. Below is a list of things you can use for reducing anxiety/stress.

Chamomile

If you have a jittery moment, a cup of chamomile tea might help calm you down. Some compounds in chamomile (Matricaria recutita) bind to the same brain receptors as drugs like valium.

You can also take it as a supplement, typically standardized to contain 1.2% apigenin (an active ingredient), along with dried chamomile flowers. In one study at the University of Pennsylvania Medical Center, in Philadelphia, patients with generalized anxiety disorder (GAD) who took chamomile supplements for eight weeks had a significant decrease in anxiety symptoms compared to patients taking placebo.

L-theanine (or green tea)

They say Japanese Buddhist monks could meditate for hours, both alert and relaxed. One reason may have been an amino acid in their green tea called L-theanine, says Mark Blumenthal, of the American Botanical Council.

Research shows that L-theanine helps curb a rising heart rate and blood pressure, and a few small human studies have found that it reduces anxiety. In one study, anxiety-prone subjects were calmer and more focused during a test if they took 200 milligrams of L-theanine beforehand.

You can get that much L-theanine from green tea, but you'll have to drink many cups—as few as five, as many as 20.

Hops

Yes, it's in beer, but you won't get the tranquilizing benefits of the bitter herb hops (Humulus lupulus) from a brew. The sedative compound in hops is a volatile oil, so you get it in extracts and tinctures—and as aromatherapy in hops pillows.

"It's very bitter, so you don't see it in tea much, unless combined with chamomile or mint," says Blumenthal. Hops is often used as a sedative, to promote sleep, often with another herb, valerian. Note: don't take sedative herbs if you are taking a prescription tranquilizer or sedative, and let your doctor know any supplements you are taking.

Valerian

Some herbal supplements reduce anxiety without making you sleepy (such as L-theanine), while others are sedatives. Valerian (Valeriana officinalis) is squarely in the second category. It is a sleep aid, for insomnia. It contains sedative compounds; the German government has approved it as a treatment for sleep problems.

Valerian smells kind of nasty, so most people take it as a capsule or tincture, rather than a tea. If you want to try it, take it in the evening—not before you go to work! Valerian is often combined with other sedative herbs such as hops, chamomile, and lemon balm.

Lemon balm

Named after the Greek word for "honey bee," lemon balm (Melissa officinalis), has been used at least since the Middle Ages to reduce stress and anxiety, and help with sleep. In one study of healthy volunteers, those who took standardized lemon balm extracts (600 mg) were more calm and alert than those who took a placebo.

While it's generally safe, be aware that some studies have found that taking too much can actually make you more anxious. So follow directions and start with the smallest dose. Lemon balm is sold as a tea, capsule, and tincture. It's often combined with other calming herbs such as hops, chamomile, and valerian.

Exercise

Exercise is safe, good for the brain, and a powerful antidote to depression and anxiety, both immediately and in the long term. "If you exercise on a regular basis, you'll have more self-esteem and feel healthier," says Drew Ramsey, MD, Assistant Clinical Professor of Psychiatry at New York-Presbyterian Hospital, Columbia University, who blogs atwww.DrewRamseyMD.com.

"One of the major causes of anxiety is worrying about illness and health, and that dissipates when you are fit."

The 21-minute cure

Twenty-one minutes: that's about how long it takes for exercise to reliably reduce anxiety, studies show, give or take a minute. "If you're really anxious and you hop on a treadmill, you will feel more calm after the workout," Dr. Ramsey says.

"I generally ask my patients to spend 20 to 30 minutes in an activity that gets their heart rate up, whether it's a treadmill or elliptical or stair stepping—anything you like. If you rowed in college, get back to rowing. If you don't exercise, start taking brisk walks."

Passionflower

In spite of the name, this herb won't help you in love. It's a sedative; the German government has approved it for nervous restlessness. Some studies find that it can reduce symptoms of anxiety as effectively as prescription drugs. It's often used for insomnia.

Like other sedatives, it can cause sleepiness and drowsiness, so don't take it—or valerian, hops, kava, lemon balm, or other sedative herbs—when you are also taking a prescription sedative.

Be careful about using more than one sedative herb at a time, and don't take passionflower for longer than one month at a time.

Lavender

The intoxicating (but safe) aroma of lavender (Lavandula hybrida) may be an "emotional" anti-inflammatory. In one study, Greek dental patients were less anxious if the waiting room was scented with lavender oil. In a Florida study, students who inhaled lavender oil scent before an exam had less anxiety—although some students said it made their minds "fuzzy" during the test.

In one German study, a specially formulated lavender pill (not available in the U.S.) was shown to reduce anxiety symptoms in people with Generalized Anxiety Disorder (GAD) as effectively as lorazepam (brand name: Ativan), an anti-anxiety medication in the same class as valium.

Hold your breath!

Ok, let it out now. We're not recommending that you turn blue, but yoga breathing has been shown to be effective in lowering stress and anxiety. In his bestselling 2011 book *Spontaneous Happiness*, Andrew Weil, MD, introduced a classic yoga breathing technique he calls the 4-7-8 breath.

One reason it works is that you can't breathe deeply and be anxious at the same time. To do the 4-7-8 breath, exhale completely through your mouth, then inhale through your nose for a count of four. Hold your breath for a count of seven. Now let it out slowly through your mouth for a count of eight. Repeat at least twice a day.

Eat something, quick

"Almost universally, people get more anxious and irritable when they are hungry," says Dr. Ramsey, co-author of *The Happiness Diet*. "When you get an anxiety attack, it may mean your blood sugar is dropping. The best thing to do is to have a quick sustaining snack, like a handful of walnuts, or a piece of dark chocolate, along with a glass of water or a nice cup of hot tea."

In the long term, diet is key to reducing anxiety, says Dr. Ramsey. His advice: eat a whole-foods, plant-based diet with carefully selected meat and seafood, plenty of leafy greens (such as kale) to get folate, and a wide variety of phytonutrients to help reduce anxiety.

Eat breakfast

Stop starving yourself, advises Dr. Ramsey. "Many people with anxiety disorders skip breakfast. I recommend that people eat things like eggs, which are a satiating and filling protein, and are nature's top source of choline. Low levels of choline are associated with increased anxiety." I use a wholefood meal replacement shake that includes a variety of branch chain aminoacids that help raise serotonin (the happiness hormone) levels.

Eat omega-3s

You know fish oils are good for the heart, and perhaps they protect against depression. Add anxiety to the list. In one study, students who took 2.5 milligrams a day of mixed omega-3 fatty acids for 12 weeks had less anxiety before an exam than students taking placebo.

Experts generally recommend that you get your omega-3s from food whenever possible. Oily, cold-water fishes like salmon are the best sources of the fatty acids; a six-ounce piece of grilled wild salmon contains about 3.75 grams.

Other good choices: anchovies, sardines, and mussels. I use a supplement twice daily in addition to my already healthy diet.

Stop catastrophizing

When you're attacked by anxiety, it's easy to get into a mind set known as "catastrophic thinking" or "catastrophizing." Your mind goes to the bad, terrible, really horrible, just unbearable things and what if they really do happen? "You think, 'This could really ruin my life,'" says Dr. Ramsey.

Instead, take a few deep breaths, walk around the block, and consider the real probability that this problem will really spin out into catastrophe. How likely is it that you'll lose your job, never talk to your sister again, go bankrupt?

Chances are a catastrophic outcome is a lot less likely than you think when you're consumed with anxiety. "Very few events really change the trajectory of your life," says Dr. Ramsey.

Get hot

Ever wonder why you feel so relaxed after a spell in the sauna or a steam room? Heating up your body reduces muscle tension and anxiety, research finds. Sensations of warmth may alter neural circuits that control mood, including those that affect the neurotransmitter serotonin. Warming up may be one of the ways that exercise—not to mention curling up by a fire with a cozy cup of tea—boosts mood.

As one group of researchers put it, "Whether lying on the beach in the midday sun on a Caribbean island, grabbing a few minutes in the sauna or spa after work, or sitting in a hot bath or Jacuzzi in the evening, we often associate feeling warm with a sense of relaxation and wellbeing."

Take a 'forest bath'

The Japanese call it *Shinrin-yoku,* literally "forest bath." You and I know it as a walk in the woods. Japanese researchers measured body changes in people who walked for about 20 minutes in a beautiful forest, with the woodsy smells and the sounds of a running stream.

The forest bathers had lower stress hormone levels after their walk than they did after a comparable walk in an urban area. I have and still use this strategy with my son and now with my grandkids.

Learn mindfulness meditation

Mindfulness meditation, originally a Buddhist practice but now a mainstream therapy, is particularly effective in treating anxiety, says Teresa M. Edenfield, Ph.D., a clinical psychologist in the Veterans Administration Medical Center in Durham, N.C., who often uses it to treat anxiety patients. "The act of practicing mindful awareness allows one to experience the true essence of each moment as it really occurs, rather than what is expected or feared," she says.

How to begin? You can start by simply "paying attention to the present moment, intentionally, with curiosity, and with an effort to attend non-judgmentally," Edenfield says.

Breathe and question

To stay mindful, ask yourself simple questions while practicing breathing exercises, Edenfield suggests. "Sit in a comfortable place, close your eyes, and focus on how your breath feels coming in and out of your body. Now ask yourself silent questions while focusing on the breath."

What is the temperature of the air as it enters your nose? How does your breath feel different as it leaves your body? How does the air feel as it fills your lungs?

Give yourself credit

Are you having anxious thoughts? Congratulations. You're aware of your emotional state, and that awareness is the first step in reducing anxiety, says Edenfield.

"Remember to give yourself credit for being aware that you are having anxious thoughts, and probably body changes. This is truly a skill of mindfulness that must be learned, and is essential in making the next steps of intervening through strategies such as positive self-talk, cognitive reframing, or the use of mindfulness or relaxation strategies."[30]

[26]http://www.isagenixhealth.net/your-brain-on-adaptogens/
[27, 28] Psychiatry Research May 30, 2015: 227(1); 46-51
[29]HCP Live August 26, 2015
[30]http://www.health.com/health/gallery/0,,20669377,00.html

Chapter 4

FEAR AND ANXIETY

Fear and anxiety are two sides of the same coin. In fact, anxiety or worry are just a couple of the many faces of fear.

How do you forget fear?

Fear is the awareness of danger, and it's a useful thing to experience whenever a real threat exists.

There's the catch. How much real, life-threatening danger actually exists in your life? Very little. People fear public speaking, but where's the potential for danger? People fear for their jobs, but in this affluent society, how does the loss of a job constitute real danger?

There's an acronym for fear that I've used for years: False Expectations Appearing Real. Become aware that most of the fear you experience in this rich society of ours is probably false, that your expectations of danger may not be grounded in reality. Should this be the case, change those expectations.

It's simple: Expect better from yourself and from the world around you. Act as if these expectations will be fulfilled. The fear will dissipate, anticipation will grow, and you may even enjoy yourself.

Yes, you might just get what you expect. Stranger things have happened.

Remember: Your thoughts creates emotion. Take small, consistent and purposeful steps that lead you away from fear and toward enthusiasm, excitement and enjoyment. Start immediately. You'll put fear on the run before the day is done.

With the onslaught of violence, negativity and threats arriving through various news channels like TV, radio news, newspapers or social media we get constantly bombarded with bad news. Our brains are getting programed to negativity and in the process are more likely to focus on negativity in the future. You will always see all the bad first, hear the bad first and talk about it too. So, I decided to do something about that. Yes, I still need to some extend know what is going on but usually I can't change it. I now briefly skim over the news to stay in the loop as to what is going on and I purposefully focus on positive news, on ways that can make our life better, or bring about positive change. I train my brain to look for positivity in all aspects of life.

Shawn Achor found in his research that only 25% of your success is actually dictated by your intelligence or skills. The remaining 75% is dictated by 3 elements that you need to learn:

1. Optimism, how you feel about yourself and your abilities to be successful
2. Your social connections
3. How you perceive stress. Do you perceive an incident as a treat or a challenge?

It appears that by learning how to shift your mind and think about any fear as a challenge rather than a threat you may reduce any negative effects from stress by over 20%. When we think about STRESS as a threat it actually shuts down our brain function as well as our immune system. Once you learn that any threat is just a challenge or test you need to pass or overcome, the brain switches to a positive mindset that actually improves your performance, your success rate, and your health outcome significantly. By focusing not on what is broken, but rather concentrating on what is working you will be able to create many positive successful realities in your life. Mr. Achor believes that happiness is one of the most important advantages in our modern economy.

Motivation (and the many faces of fear)

You *can* motivate yourself. It's easy to do. There are two reasons why anyone does anything: to avoid pain and to gain pleasure. We're either moving toward something we want, or we're moving away from something we don't want.

For example: when you do something unpleasant or painful, it's because you expect to gain something—in the long run—that's pleasurable enough to compensate for your pain. Studying to become a doctor or working at a job you hate in order to pay for your dream home are a couple of things that come to mind.

High achievers are people who take action in all circumstances. They do this because they know that greater rewards will be earned in the long run. They've given themselves enough good reasons to pursue their dreams that they're compelled to action. And that's the secret: you can overcome the many faces of fear and reach high levels of motivation just by giving yourself enough good reasons to act!

Exercise:

Write down three pleasurable things you expect to gain when you adopt the techniques offered in 60 SECONDS TO SUCCESS:

1.

2.

3.

Write down three painful (or unpleasant) things you expect to avoid when you adopt the techniques offered here:

1.

2.

3.

Come up with at least two new reasons every day for feeling excited, enthusiastic and energetic about the future. Write these things down and review the entire list every morning. Keep at it until you have 60 reasons for taking action on a daily basis. You'll be motivated! I was.

Write down what excites you today:

1.

2.

Feel Amazing and Look Even Better

Come up with at least two good motivational questions you can ask yourself every morning when you wake up:

1.

2.

(Hint: These questions should inspire positive emotions that get you taking immediate action.)

1. Will this behaviour help me get what I want?

    a) Are these thoughts helping me get what I want from life?
    b) Are these feelings going to help me move closer to my goals?
    c) If I say this, will I move closer to my goals?
    d) Will this action produce results that will help me get what I want from life?
    e) What pleasant results will I experience if I go ahead with this behaviour?
    f) What unpleasant results will I experience if I go ahead with this behaviour?
    g) Are these the results I really want?

2. What can I do, right now, that will move me closer to my goals?
    a) What reasons do I have for doing this; what pleasant results will I experience, and what unpleasant results will I avoid?

3. What am I doing that isn't perfect yet, and what can I do to improve my results?

4. What could I have done to prevent this situation/event?

5. What can I do to keep it from ever happening again?

6. What have I got to be grateful for?

7. What's good about this situation?

8. How can I make this problem work for me?

9. Where's the opportunity in this situation?

The above questions are designed to focus your thoughts on what you can do instead of what you can't do. The questions can also get you taking actions more likely to move you in the direction of your goals. Pick your answers carefully. Cultivate the thoughts, feelings, words and actions most likely to get you what you want from life. Eliminate all else.

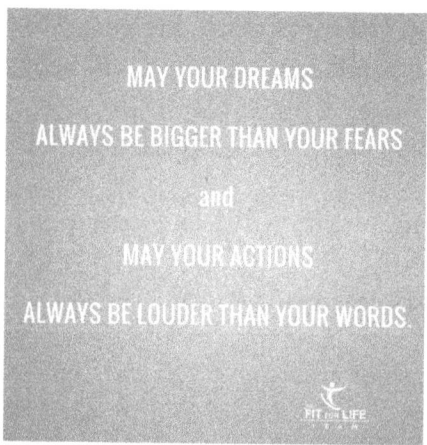

Come up with your own list of power questions. Keep adding to it (and amending it) until you end up with a set of questions you'll use on a daily basis. Ask these questions every chance you get - and watch your life change!

How do you stop worrying?

Generate lots of enthusiasm. Give no thought to success or failure. Think only of having fun with the tasks you've set for yourself. *Choose to be positive.*

Failure employs many snipers who love to strike when you're low. Worry is one of the nastiest of these henchmen. Success under fire comes to those who build strong internal reserves, who prepare themselves for their inevitable battles with such agents of adversity. Armour yourself with enthusiasm. Shield yourself with joy.

Joe Tye once said "Worry is ingratitude to God - in advance." You've got to find a way to maintain your sense of enjoyment and gratitude even while under a hail of life's bullets. Trust that your preparation and hard work will see you through. Learn to sing, dance and be merry while sweeping the floors. Find something useful in the rudeness of a customer. Look at that pay cut as the messenger of opportunity.

Become aware that the worry you're experiencing is a form of fear, an illusion of a perceived threat that may or may not happen. Transform what you're feeling by changing your expectations and your actions. Find some new behaviours that generate enthusiasm and enjoyment, and be persistent in the pursuit of them.

Remember, the only way to replace a habit is with another habit. Your daily habits will help you to overcome anything you do not like or want to change.

Dealing with anxiety

1. Repeat your worry until you're bored silly. If you had a fear of elevators, you'd get rid of it if you rode in one a thousand times in a row. At first, you would be very anxious, then less so, and eventually it would have no effect (except to make you sick of riding in an elevator). Your thought will become so familiar that it will feel normal at some point. So take the troublesome thought that's nagging at you and say it over and over, silently, slowly, for 20 minutes. It's

hard to keep your mind on a worry if you repeat it that many times. I call this the "boredom cure" for obvious reasons, but it sure beats feeling overwhelmed by anxiety.

2. Make it worse. When you try too hard to control your anxieties, you only heighten them. Instead, exaggerate them and see what happens. For instance, if you fear that your mind will go blank during a presentation, fake it intentionally in the middle of your next one. Say, "Gee, what was I just saying?" Notice how this makes no difference. It's nothing to worry about, right? I did this at a lecture once and no one raised an eyebrow. (Perhaps they weren't listening anyway!)

3. Don't fight the craziness. You may occasionally have thoughts that lead you to think you'll do something terrible ("I'm attracted to him. Does that mean I'll have an affair?") or that you're going insane (a client of mine who is an attorney kept imagining herself screaming in court). Remember—our minds are creative. Little synapses are firing away at random, and every now and then a "crazy" thought jumps out. Everyone has them. Instead of judging yours, describe it to yourself like it's a curious object on a shelf and move on.

4. Recognize false alarms. That fear of your house burning down because you left the iron on has never come true. That rapid heartbeat doesn't mean you're having a heart attack; it's your body's natural response to arousal. Many thoughts and sensations that we interpret as cues for concern—even panic—are just background noise. Think of each of them as a fire engine going to another place. You've noticed them; now let them pass by.

5. Turn your anxiety into a movie. You can let go of a worry by disconnecting yourself from it. One way is to imagine that your anxious thoughts are a show. Maybe they're a little guy in a funny hat who tap dances and sings out your worry while you sit in the audience, eating popcorn, a calm observer. Here is a fun example: if you experience anxiety to meet or face a certain person, imagine him

or her in their underwear and your perception may make you smile instead.

6. Set aside worry time. All too often we take a "Crackberry" approach to our worries: They show up unannounced, like constantly dinging e-mails, and we stop everything to address them—even if we should be doing something else. But what if you don't respond right away? Try setting aside 20 minutes every day—let's say at 4:30 p.m.—just for your worries. If you are fretting at 10 a.m., jot down the reason and resolve to think it through later. By the time 4:30 comes around, many of your troubles won't even matter anymore. And you will have spent almost an entire day anxiety-free.

7. Take your hand off the horn. You constantly check the weather before a big outdoor event. You replay that clumsy comment you made, wishing you could take it back. And, yes, you honk your horn in traffic. When you desperately try to take command of things that can't be controlled, you're like the swimmer who panics and slaps at the water, screaming. It gets you nowhere. Instead, imagine that you are floating along on the water with your arms spread out, looking up to the sky. It's a paradox, but when you surrender to the moment, you actually feel far more in control.

8. Breathe it out. You may notice that when your body is tense, you hold your breath. Focusing on breathing is a common but effective technique for calming the nerves. Where is your breath now, and where is your mind? Bring them together. Listen to the movement of your breath. Does your mind wander somewhere else? Call it back. Concentrate only on breathing in and out, beginning and ending, breath to breath, moment to moment.

9. Make peace with time. When you're a worrier, everything can feel like an emergency. But notice this about all your anxious arousal: it's temporary. Every feeling of panic comes to an end, every concern eventually wears itself out, every so-called emergency seems to

evaporate. Ask yourself, "How will I feel about this in a week or a month?" This one, too, really will pass.

10. Don't let your worries stop you from living your life. Many of them will turn out to be false, and the consequences of your anxiety—less sleep, a rapid pulse, a little embarrassment—are just inconveniences when it comes down to it. What can you still do even if you feel anxious? Almost anything.[31]

[31]http://www.realsimple.com/health/mind-mood/emotional-health/ten-ways-to-cope-with-anxiety

Chapter 5

BELIEVE IN YOURSELF

What do I deserve?

"Happiness is when I feel good about myself without feeling the need for anyone else's approval." – *unknown*

    Have you ever thought about it? What ... do ... I ... deserve? Many people do not give themselves permission to believe in a future of abundance: abundant joy, abundant income, abundant health and abundant love. I'm sure you can build a longer list if you will sit down and do it. The thing is that these listed items already exist and await you, free of judgement. They do not think, and as such there is no "I deserve" or "I do not deserve." There is NO real reason one person deserves more than another. You deserve as much as anyone! Your thoughts and the actions you take because of your thoughts determine the outcome. Remember, how much money you make, where you live, or your family situation became reality because of the choices you made or someone in your family made for you. Yet these facts only account for 10% of your happiness, while the remaining 90% of your happiness comes from how you process information and how that affects your thoughts, which ultimately trigger what you do next. If you feel you don't deserve more joy, better health or an abundant income, then it's all on you. You will not strive for more and thus you will never achieve it. You may not even consider any solution or opportunity that presents itself. So set some goals and go for abundance in all areas of your life.

How do other people perceive me?

Essentially it does not really matter what others think of you. The only thing that matters is what do you think of yourself. Do you feel who you are and what you do and say is right and authentically you? What you think others are thinking about you may actually hold you back from your potential and who you really are. Besides, have you ever thought about who the people are who do not like the way you are, talk or look? Are they the people who inspire you to be as successful as they are? Are they the people who have ever taken risks themselves? Are they happy and supportive? Or are those people conforming to everything and hanging their sails always in the direction the wind is blowing? Are they really unique themselves, and using their gifts in a positive way?

A good example are pop icons like Madonna or Lady Gaga, who had the courage to live their wildest dreams of themselves in broad view, and millions of people admire that about them. Most people are afraid of living and behaving like that. We prefer to blend in when we are actually made to stand out. We are all unique and bring unique gifts and talents to the world.

The only purpose a question like how other people perceive you can serve you is to help refine your picture of yourself. If people think you talk too much, and you feel that in fact this is valuable feedback to improve yourself, this is a good reason for you to practice and improve your communication skills. It is not meant to be a negative experience or the beginning of a pity party. Using the feedback that your friends and co-workers think that you talk too much is something you can change if you feel that to be valid. It is valuable feedback that may help you to improve yourself.

Believing you're not good enough, smart enough, strong enough

How would you know that you are not smart enough, good enough or strong enough if you never tested it in the first place? Maybe you have these beliefs because someone told you. Maybe you were raised that way, or a teacher once said this to you.

Your beliefs create your reality. Once you shift that thought and replace it with the belief that you are here on this planet because of your uniqueness and your specific traits, talents and strengths to accomplish or create something of significance that makes you happy and may even contribute to someone else's benefit, you will only be contemplating how to improve your personal gifts and use them in a most efficient way.

What other people tell you about your abilities is only based on their perception and their beliefs in themselves. Some very successful people actually used such feedback to show everyone what they were capable of doing. They wanted to prove them wrong, which enforced a strong belief in themselves, that lead to unprecedented actions and to their ultimate success.

Rita Davenport is one of these people. She grew up in extreme poverty, with several teachers telling her that she did not have any college potential. She not only graduated from college, but despite a speech impediment became one of the most sought-after motivational speakers. She had her own TV show interviewing hundreds of celebrities and later served for 10 years as the president of a very successful international company, Arbonne International.

Having low self-esteem based on past experiences, on upbringing, being influenced by others and feeling redundant when losing a job

Changing one's self-talk can lead to the development of new beliefs that are not as limiting as the current ones. Harnessing the power of your mind, increasing your ability to feel good about yourself, learning how to make better choices and changing the day-to-day results of your life—all these things can be achieved by asking yourself specific questions.

So, let's try and ask yourself these questions:

1. Have you been blaming someone or something for the state of your life? Have you been blaming yourself? Blaming anyone for something that happened in your life is easy yet not very productive. Does it change your situation in any way? Does it serve you in creating positivity in some way? Does it help you in finding a solution to your current dilemma?
2. If you had the opportunity to start all over, what would you do differently? How would you do it? What steps could you take today to get yourself moving toward your dreams again?
3. You've been told you're going to die tomorrow: Will you still do the things you'd planned for today? If not, what would you do? Why?
4. What would you like to be remembered for?

How did you do? Were the questions difficult to answer or were they easy to answer? Can you see how they begin the process of taking responsibility, of choosing to live your life, rather than letting life live you? Do you recognize that these questions change your focus, to evaluate where you are in life and to get you looking at your goals and dreams with renewed purpose?

Take another look at those questions. Why? Questions make you think. They force you to define your ideas and beliefs, a process that can result in the deep-seated conviction, the sense of purpose, the burning desire that's the key to consistent action and, ultimately, to success. If you aren't prepared to ask and honestly answer many of these questions, you won't be able to create lasting change in your life.

Don't be like the average. The sad truth is that most people won't do what it takes to create lasting change in their live either because they see their challenges as insurmountable, or they act like there's a secret that successful people have access to, but that's carefully hidden from them. And it's not true. Your dreams are achievable. You just have to take consistent decisive actions, find alternative resources, and look in new directions, finding new ways of going about things.

This section of the book is designed to answer the question "How?" How do you end the frustration and unhappiness caused by unfulfilled dreams? How do you get yourself to do the things that will produce the results you want? How do you get yourself to keep on taking those actions? Read on, do the exercises, complete the questions, and you'll find the answers you're looking for.

Bob Proctor once said "I want to live until I die, and age has nothing to do with it."

Once you decide that you want to live a happy, purposeful and successful life, you can find out how to do that. The journey will look different for each of us. Think of it as climbing a mountain. Reaching the peak of your personal success means finding the way that makes the most sense for you. The way is different for each person. Some use serpentines to get to the top; others use the harder but direct way.

Success and the happiness that comes by achieving is never a constant. You achieve a certain goal, and enjoy the gratification that comes with it for a while. At some point you look for more, set another higher goal to experience a new reward and find happiness in achieving again. Ambition, passion and joy are the drivers to keep you going. It is also what advances science, technology, the arts, and the way society evolves.

Children have that ability from birth. They want to move; first they crawl, then walk, then run, then learn how to ride a bike, and later how to drive a car.

Athletes are never discouraged to achieve a new best or new heights because no one else has accomplished them yet. On the contrary, athletes are constantly looking for new training methods, theories or advances in science. They are compelled to become better than anyone else before them.

Scientists never stop dreaming of finding new solutions, advancements, or discoveries. They use their current knowledge as a solid foundation, or are even more daring by taking brand new unconventional approaches to find simpler ways for advancement that no one else thought possible.

Having a goal and shooting for it is essential to success. The Wright Brothers are a great example of that. They knew what they wanted. They wanted to fly! Everybody thought they were out of their minds. Flying was only for the birds and certain insects. It was all everyone knew then. The brothers took inspiration from the birds. They wanted to understand what they needed to do to fly. Did they crash? Did they get hurt? Did they care about what other folks thought about them? Did they lose a ton of money? Did they invent the first flying machine? Did their efforts, persistence, enthusiasm, courage, imagination help them achieve their goal and dream to fly? Their success changed the way we travel today. It benefited all of us and encouraged future generations to advance and improve on their discoveries. It even compelled us to think about space travel, to places not even birds would fly.

I once heard a definition of success that stuck in my mind: Success is the pursuit of a worthwhile goal. I like that. Follow your dreams and you become successful. Pursue your idea of what's worthwhile for you, do what you love to do, live your dream—and you become successful. It doesn't matter if you achieve a certain place in life or not. The effort you make is what's important: the process of becoming more, of challenging yourself, of trying to find the limits of your potential will always propel you further.

Success is *making* the voyage of discovery.

We are all different in our approach to lasting happiness. Each of us has different goals and dreams and is on a different *journey* through life.

I love to travel to expand my mind, learn more from different cultures, experience and appreciate the wonders and beauty of foreign landscapes. Another way to have a similar experience is through imagination. When I read about places I'd like to visit, I dream about how it may feel to be there. Just imagine the sights you see along the way, the new experiences you have, the people you meet, the thoughts and emotions and conversations you have, the discoveries you make are why you have dreams to begin with. Dreams aren't a way of escaping real life—as some people would have you think. Dreams are a vehicle made for the sole purpose of delivering you to that part of life you should have been experiencing all along: the part you enjoy!

What are you dreaming about? Think about that for a moment. Why are you excited about it? How would your life change if your dream ever became reality? How would that make you feel? What is holding you back from going after it?

Dreams that excite you are messages from your soul to remind you of what is possible for you, what you are capable of and what your soul desires to experience and achieve during your lifetime. Do not ignore it! Some people call this desire and feeling to follow your heart. It is something that makes you feel good, has you excited looking for ways to make it happen.

A tool, and a fun thing to do to keep your dream vivid and in your mind all the time is to create a vision board. Fill it with pictures and statements that describe your goals and dreams. Make it colourful and hang it in a place where you will see it every day. Some of my friends keep it on their bathroom mirror, others have it on their desk. Jack Canfield offers a beautiful vision board set you can order online but you can also just use some cardboard, magazine clippings, coloured pencils and markers. Be creative and have fun with it! Once you have achieved several of your goals, you may have to create a new vision board. Your board may need updating every few years as new goals become apparent.

Essentially, following your dream is like planning a trip you always wanted to take. You look for ways to get to your destination. You want to learn more about your destination by researching it, talking to people who have been there already and ask them for input and advice. You evaluate different ways to get there and then pick the one that makes the most sense to you.

To make this a worthwhile endeavour, I advise you to write down your goals. Establish WHY reaching your goal is important to you. Clinical psychologist, Dr. Gail Matthews has studied goal achievement. Her research found that those participants who wrote down their goals achieved significantly more than those who did not.

In fact Dr. Matthews' research demonstrated that:
- 43% of the participants who had written goals also achieved them.
- If the participants formulated action commitments in addition to their written goals, their success rate grew to 64%.
- Once the participant not only had written goals and formulated action commitments, but also shared their goals and commitments with a supportive friend who would receive their weekly progress report, the success rate of achieving their goal climbed to 76%.
- Not everyone has financial goals but I found the following Harvard MBA study from 1989 remarkable, as it supports the importance of written goals to achieve success. Why do 3% of Harvard MBAs make ten times as much as the other 97 percent combined? Mark McCormack wrote about it in his book "What They Don't Teach you in the Harvard Business School".[32]

In 1979 Harvard asked the graduates of their MBA program about their goals.
- 84% had no specific goals at all.
- 13% had goals but never wrote them down.
- 3% had clear, written goals AND plans to accomplish them

In 1989 they surveyed the same graduates.
- 13% of the class who had goals were earning on average twice as much as the 84% who had no goals at all.
- And the 3% who had clear, written goals were earning on average ten times as much as the other 97% combined.

- Unclear goals will create road blocks and never help you achieve your goals. Think about it in terms of weight loss. An example of a not very valuable goal would be "I want to lose weight." Many people want that. Who wouldn't? A much better example of clear and concise goal would be "I want to lose 10 lbs in 2 months." Having a concrete and measurable goal makes it more likely to achieve it because you can track your progress along the way.

Andrew Carnegie once said "If you want to be happy, set a goal that commands your thoughts, liberates your energy and inspires your hopes."

Professor Locke also found that your goal should also be challenging so that once you achieve it you feel good about yourself. Going back to the weight loss example, would you honestly feel good about yourself if you committed to losing 1 lb in 2 months? Essentially you could just not do anything for 7 weeks and then just not eat at all the last day. Your goals have to be something worth fighting for, that will drive your performance to achieve them. The more difficult your goal, the more effort you exert to achieve it and the better you'll feel about your achievement.

Once the reason for achieving your goal is so compelling that it drives you enough to go through eventual challenges and road blocks your desire to achieve it will propel you towards your goal. For example, I have coached people to reach their weight loss goal because they had a very personal reason WHY they wanted it. Some wanted to be a good example for their kids. Their results would ultimately also improve the health and life of their children. Another friend wanted to be able to fit into the harness of a skydiving school. He had always dreamed about parachuting but did not meet the weight limit for the harness. I once met a lady whose child was too embarrassed to have her mom come to teacher interviews. All her classmates were making jokes about how big her mom was.

Professor Locke also states that with constructive feedback, evaluating what works and what does not, you will be more effective in reaching your goal. We use Facebook groups, coaching calls and incentives to follow up on progress, tweak your personal approach and measure your results.

And finally, if you are pursuing a very lofty, big goal it may help you to break your journey down into smaller, more easily achievable intermittent goals. This approach helps you to not get frustrated, overwhelmed and give up too soon. You can celebrate the smaller achievements along the way and build on that experience. It keeps you happier and motivates you to go further each time.

Aren't you pursuing what you really want (or thinking about pursuing it) because you want to add more excitement, joy and variety to your life? Don't you expect the achievement of your dream to increase your level of satisfaction, to provide you with a sense of accomplishment and to make you feel more alive? Now, what if I told you that you're going to experience all of those feelings long before you reach your destination, that you become successful just by making the journey! Your decision to take the necessary steps towards your goals will empower you, will keep you thinking about the outcome and open your eyes and mind to new ways to get there. When you follow your heart, you travel through life happily, with a sense of purpose, and obstacles just become challenges you want to conquer and overcome. With each step you take towards your goal you'll become more confident, more daring and more successful.

Sure, reaching a goal and achieving a dream will make you feel good. And why not? The end of an adventure is reason for celebration and reflection. Your accomplishment became possible because you also used your skills, refined and improved them along the way. Take the time to celebrate your success.

So often people do not even get started on this road of joy and fulfillment because they believe that they are not capable, deserving, good enough, skilled enough, smart enough, and so forth. Once you stop dreaming or never even get started, your gifts will lay dormant; your mind and soul will not be able to grow, expand and enjoy. Your gift of life will be wasted and may expire early. Cherish that gift; value the opportunity to be the best you can be. Do not waste it! You owe it to yourself, to your loved ones, to the people who depend on you, and first and foremost you owe it to God, who gave you life in the first place.

Keep in mind that this goal you've reached is only one destination, a small part of the entire voyage that makes up your life. Each goal is a tool, a way to expand your experience, make you smarter, better, stronger, happier. Take a little time to savour your victory, be grateful for all the experiences good and bad. They are all happening to teach you new skills and sharpen the talents you already posess. Consider the people who helped you along the way, and share your gained wisdom, your new knowledge with those who can benefit. Then start planning your next trip!

Challenge yourself. See how many adventures you can have while on this journey we call life...

I have a friend who has stood on a mountain at the top of the world, sang on-stage with a quartet of beautiful women in Florida, tracked a moose in a blizzard, fished for Char on an uninhabited island in the Arctic Ocean, drank wine and savoured cheese on a knoll in rural New York on a perfect summer day, played guitar with professional musicians while waiting for a train in Moncton, jumped from a cliff into the river that runs through Elora Gorge, Ontario, watched actors stage a gunfight on the streets of Rawhide in the middle of a flash flood, flew in a Hercules aircraft, stood eye-to-eye with a musk ox, owned and drove a baby-blue '52 Chevy and worked—simply for the fun of it—as a model and a private investigator.

Why and how did he do those things? He believes in packing as much living as he can into the time he's got left on this earth. And I can assure you this is one of the secrets to a rich and fulfilling existence.

And speaking of success secrets ... Have you heard of those people who keep travel journals? Get yourself one. But rather than filling it with descriptions of sights and sounds, use it to keep track of your successes. Why? The success most people talk about is nothing more than a full scorecard.

Why is a full scorecard a big deal? When you keep a running list of your achievements, you give yourself a powerful tool, a way of measuring what you've already done. The score card is a positive reminder of how well you've done so far and how far you could still go.

Get a scorecard. Fill the thing up. Study it, and allow yourself to be inspired to even greater achievements. Know that if you're making regular entries in your journal/scorecard, then you're busy achieving fulfilling your potential, and it tells you whether or not you're getting to where you want to go instead of worrying, complaining or procrastinating. No entries? You may not think too much about what you have done so far and may not feel the importance for recognizing it. We all have done something worthwhile, even mistakes count because they teach us. That's all important information! Because taking action towards something you want is often the only difference between successful people and those who aren't.

**Success is concentrating on doing something,
not worrying about why you can't.**

I've never heard of a successful Olympic calibre athlete who thought he or she couldn't win. These stellar individuals know exactly what they want, and they're busy pursuing those goals. Top-notch athletes don't have room for "I can't" in their lives. Their entire focus is on the achievement of THE DREAM. So, why don't you follow their example? Be the champion of your life: decide what you want, know it's possible for you to achieve, then put your entire focus on making it happen. Don't fear, and follow your plan.

Children are also a great example. They want to walk and get up without any fear or complaint when they still tumble advancing from crawling to standing to walking to running.

My personal philosophy is that we will only be confronted with challenges that we can overcome. They come up to teach to us something in some way. Maybe we are forced to study a new way, learn a new skill or learn from earlier mistakes, find a different approach, or to use someone else's help and learn how to work in groups or partnerships. This philosophy has helped me to never get discouraged but feel compelled to move ahead on my journey.

Know that your journey is unique. We are all unique in our own way, with different strengths and weaknesses, gifts and talents, and different goals that make us happy. Comparing yourself to others will not help, nor would it make any sense.

Once you've recognized that it's possible to achieve your dreams, the key is to focus all your thoughts and energy on how you're going to do it, then get yourself to follow through.

Remember, you become successful by taking the voyage. The only way you'll get to the destinations you dream about is by taking consistent and purposeful action.

That's why I mentioned the importance of concentrating on how you can do something, rather than on why you can't. So many people defeat themselves. They say "I could never do that. I don't have the skills. I don't have the brains. I don't have the money." Honestly, those are all just excuses because you are afraid of failure. You can do almost anything—if you want to do it badly enough. The skills you need can be learned, or you can enlist the help of someone who already has those skills.

Remember: you're going to run into enough obstacles in your lifetime, so why go looking for them? Wouldn't you agree that it's far more productive to give yourself a lot of reasons for chasing your dreams? The more reasons you give yourself for pursuing your dreams, the stronger will become your desire to achieve them. Keep working at it long enough, and your desire will actually become a sense of certainty that your dreams will come true. When this happens, nothing can stop you!

Pay attention to what you think. Your thoughts are powerful. They change your "vibration." As an energy healer I work with people's energy to optimize the way they feel, heal from injury or illness, or recover from trauma or negative incidents. This is a simple and brief way explaining what vibration means.

We are all energy. Energy keeps us warm, makes us move, think and feel. Our thoughts, experiences, and feelings about something or someone have an effect on how our energy flows through our body. It shows on the outside in the way we react to circumstances and what we say and it is expressed in our body language, and how we appeal to others. Positive thinking, optimism, honesty, integrity, love, forgiveness, happiness, optimal physical and mental health, all affect how our energy flows and vibrates. The higher your vibration, the more others feel attracted to you. Obviously, your attraction rate (vibration) can be helpful or hindering in your success. Taking care of your body, your mind and your thoughts is critical. A positive outlook will make your journey a lot easier.

There's this little thing some people call self-fulfilling prophecy that's based on the concept that what you think has power over you. Now you know why this idea has validity.

Do your best to concentrate on how you can do a thing, never on why you can't. Thinking about why your dreams can't come true will increase the likelihood of that outcome. Conversely, putting your focus on what you can do to achieve your dreams must improve your chances of success.

Dare to dream! There are always ways to create the future you want—use your imagination, perseverance and all the resources available to you. Accept responsibility for yourself. Take action!

**If you want your dreams to come true,
it's up to you to make them happen!**

Successful people don't just dream—they act. Successful people take charge and create the outcomes they want. These people have something inside that drives them to do whatever's necessary to achieve their goals. What is it? What do they do to make their dreams happen? And can you do the same thing to create the results you want?

Absolutely. In fact, I've already given you the answer to the above questions. The solution is so simple you'll probably have trouble accepting the enormous impact it can have on your life. You will be successful, if you start thinking about what you honestly want to achieve, even if it seems so unreal. Imagine it so vividly, feel the excitement, that you'll want to follow it through to completion, no matter what happens.

Give yourself some compelling reasons why this is important to you, write it down, then follow your plan by taking the necessary action, and stay focused. Let yourself want something badly enough that it becomes an obsession, when you wake up in the morning with the desire to take action towards your goal. Once you take action, don't stop until you achieve the results you want. It's possible. You can do it. Dare to dream!

We don't all need to entertain the incredible dreams of a Henry Ford or a Thomas Edison or a Steve Jobs (but it helps). We just need something that means a lot to us.

Does this make sense? If you're scared to death of being poor, you'll eventually find a way to stay out of the grip of poverty, nurturing dreams of wealth until you figure out how to make it happen. If you're excited enough about owning a certain car, you'll do what it takes to secure a loan or save the money you need to buy it—even if it takes ten or fifteen years. On a simpler level, when you're thirsty enough, you'll pull away from that great television show and get a drink from the fridge. When you want a haircut, you go to a hair stylist or a barber. Achievement is all about cause and effect, action and result.

You see, it's not so important what you do, as it is that you do something. If you can make yourself want something strongly enough, cultivating the need for it until it becomes a burning desire, visualizing your dream so clearly that you'll take action on a daily basis and find a way , so you'll get it.

**If you want a better life,
you must do the things that will give you a better life.**

Suffering from depression

This is a real problem for millions of people.

Sometimes depression is situational; it's a kind of despair that's brought on by your situation. The way to deal with depression is to learn certain life skills to change your focus.

Other times depression can be physiological; doctors have pretty much determined that certain imbalances of chemicals in the brain cause depression. In this case a combination of life skills, a change in your lifestyle and nutrition will be helpful, and sometimes medication is necessary to combat the depression.

The bottom line with depression is that people who haven't suffered from depression will not, cannot, understand what you're going through. So, I'm going to turn this section of the book over to a friend of mine who suffers from bi-polar disorder brought about by chemical imbalances in the brain, and who also has occasional schizophrenic episodes. In fact he also went through years of clinical depression, the most serious type of depression there is.

Depression, serious depression, is like being possessed. Someone else takes over your actions and pushes you to the back of your mind where you watch in horror as your pain is taken out on loved ones, as your job is left behind as you go home one day, bury your head under the pillows of your bed and refuse to come out. You cry and cry and cry. Thoughts of suicide run through your mind, even though you, the captive, would never think of such a thing. But you're not in charge here; some demon is hell-bent on destroying your life. Your family, hurt beyond belief, begins to withdraw their support, sending you further into an aloneness you could never have imagined possible.

Then one day, months later, you wake up and you feel great. Better than great. Your thoughts are golden. You decide that you're going to begin your own business, and ignoring your spouse's pleas you take your life savings to begin the new endeavour. Everything is going to be fine. You can wipe out the damage done while you were depressed. Just wait and see. Except … a week into your plans you take a sickening plunge as the demon resurfaces. You run home to your bedroom, slam the door, dive for the bed and refuse to come out for two weeks, except to go to the bathroom or to lay on the couch with the TV on. Not that you can concentrate. No, the TV is just noise you're using to try and keep the demon at bay.

No luck. He breaks out and you begin to dream of putting an end to him once and for all. You think of many ways to do this: cutting your throat, driving headlong into a transport truck, overdosing on the medicines your doctor has given you in an attempt to bring you back from the brink. Then something so terrible happens that you just can't take it. You break free, drive yourself to the local hospital and ask to be admitted to the psychiatric ward. The attending doctor asks why. You answer: Doctor, I not only want to kill myself; I want to kill you. I want to kill and rape until someone puts me down like a dog. And I'm afraid that I might just do it. I need to be locked up.

So they put you in the padded room, locked up like the crazed animal you are. They take you off all your meds and begin the detoxification process, preparing the ground so that they can begin again.

You stay in lock-up for four days before you come out. Then you begin to tell the nurses what has been going on. That's what you do, right? Wrong. The psychiatrist comes to you and tells you that you're scaring the nurses, that you must stop. If you can't? Then you will be sent to jail. Yes, that's right: you either find a way to control yourself or you go directly to jail.

I sit on the bed in my room and I think. I think for a long, long time. Then I look hard at the demon; he looks back at me. And then I gain an insight. If I can look at the demon, then I can also look away. I can look to the light and turn my back on the darkness. It seems too simple, but I try it. And to my surprises it works. Not perfectly, but enough for me to wrest control from the demon. He rages within me, but I refuse to pay attention. I spend my days searching for beauty and for reasons to experience joy. And as I find these things, the demon seems to shrink. Oh, he swells up at times, but now I know what to do. I do not allow him to win. Three weeks later, armed with new prescriptions meant to dampen the effects of the demon, I am released.

It's been two years. I still have depressive episodes, and mania has become more prevelant, but I battle it by spending money on little things, rather than the grandiose. And always, always, I look to the light. Especially so, when my world seems to take on an unnatural hue and I have reason to question the validity of my thoughts. These are the schizophrenic episodes mentioned earlier. When my reality fades I hang on by looking to the light. It never changes. It is the one constant in my world. You may think of the light as god, as love or as the beautiful things of the world, because it is probably a combination of all these things. I don't know. I just know it is.

Now, the reality is that the light isn't really the way out of depression. It is the pinnacle, the kicker, if you will. I have a whole arsenal of coping skills that I use every day. I was lucky: I already had these tools. They are so important. But I needed you to understand that they weren't enough, and neither were the drugs. It took something extra for me to break free of my demon. So, by all means take note of the many tools offered up in this book and those offered in other books. Use them; they will make your life easier. But also know you need outside help—the love of a spouse, the love of whatever god you believe in, the beauty that is in the world, the joy that life can bring you every day—if you look for it. These things must become your focus. Take my word for it.

Discovering and acknowledging your own qualities, traits, gifts and power

Mindful meditation:

In the Buddhist tradition and in contemplative psychotherapy training, mindfulness is nurtured through the practice of sitting meditation. Mindfulness meditation is unique (from other forms of meditation) in that it is not directed toward getting us to be different from how we already are. Instead, it helps us become aware of what is already true moment by moment. We could say that it teaches us how to be unconditionally present; that is, it helps us be present with whatever is happening, no matter what it is.

Mindfulness, paying precise, non-judgmental attention to the details of our experience as it arises and subsides, doesn't reject anything. Instead of struggling to get away from experiences we find difficult, we practice being able to be with them. Equally, we bring mindfulness to pleasant experiences as well. Perhaps surprisingly, many times we have a hard time staying simply present with happiness. We turn it into something more familiar, like worrying that it won't last or trying to keep it from fading away.

When we are mindful, we show up for our lives; we don't miss them by being distracted or wishing for things to be different. Instead, if something needs to be changed we are present enough to understand what needs to be done. Being mindful is not a substitute for actually participating in our lives and taking care of our own and others' needs.

In fact, the more mindful we are, the more skillful we can be in compassionate action.

There are three basic aspects worked with in this meditation technique: body, breath and thoughts. First, we relate with the body. This includes how we set up the environment. Since we use meditation in preparing ourselves to work with others, we use an eyes-open practice. That makes what we have in front of us a factor in our practice. Very few people can dedicate a whole room to their meditation practice, so they choose a corner of a room or a spot in their home where they can set up a quiet space.

Once you've picked your spot, you need to choose your seat. The point is to have a seat that is stable and not wiggling around. If you choose to sit on a chair, pick one that has a flat seat that doesn't tilt too much toward the back. If you are short, like me, you will want to put something on the floor for your feet to rest on, taking a little bit of weight. You don't want your legs dangling uncomfortably. If you are very tall, with long legs, make sure that your hips are higher than your knees, either on a chair or a cushion. If you don't do that your back will start to hurt pretty quickly.

Everybody does this a little different. Basically make sure you are comfortably seated and both your feet have contact with the ground. I just sit comfortably on my favourite chair in a place where I have peace and quiet so I am not distracted, and I like to close my eyes and focus on my body and my breath. Feel how it fills your body and how it travels through your lungs and your upper body, and when you exhale how your breath exits through the bottom of your feet. With every breath you take you can visualize the oxygen traveling through a different part of your body, or a specific organ. You can also directly guide the air you inhale with your thought to any area of your body that may be hurting or not working optimally at the time. For instance after an accident, a surgery or an injury you can bring the oxygen directly to the particular area that needs mending. If, for example, you suffer from anxiety, you feel depressed, guide your thoughts towards your heart. It is the centre of your energy. Think of your breath as a bright light that fills your heart. Imagine a white bubble above your forehead and place every worry, every fearful thought into that bubble. Stuff it all into that imaginary white "bag." When you are done just blow it away into the universe because you no longer have any use for what's in it.

Extend your gratitude to that particular part of your body that you were working on. Thank it for being so resilient, helpful and supporting your beautiful amazing body and your wellbeing. You may totally forget where you are and that you are sitting in your chair. After a while (that can be 10 minutes for one person or 1 hour for another) your mind will switch back as if waking up from a nice nap. You will feel refreshed and your mind will be clear. And several ideas may pop into your head while you practice mindfulness or right after, which may help you as a guide to some of your problems. Write them down so you can act on them later.

Some people advise to take this position and practice mindfulness this way. Try what you feel may work best for you and stick with it through a few sessions to get used to it. Take a posture that is upright but not rigid. The back is straight with the curve in the lower back that is naturally there. I was once told to imagine that my spine was a tree and to lean against it. It works for me; you can see if it works for you.

Sitting on a cushion, cross your legs comfortably in front of you. There's no need to contort yourself into an uncomfortable posture. Just simply cross your legs as you might have done as a child. Notice again that you want your hips higher than your knees. If necessary, add more height to your seat by folding up a blanket or towel.

Hands rest on the thighs, facing down. The eyes are somewhat open and the gaze rests gently on the floor in front of you, about four to six feet away. If you are closer to the wall than that, let your gaze rest on the wall wherever it lands, as if you were looking that distance in front. The gaze is not tightly focused. The idea is that whatever is in front of you is what's in front of you. Don't stare or do anything special with your gaze; just let it rest where you've set it.

Let your front be open and your back be strong.

Begin by just sitting in this posture for a few minutes in this environment. If your attention wanders away, just gently bring it back to your body and the environment. The key word here is "gently." Your mind WILL wander; that's part of what you will notice with your mindfulness: minds wander. When you notice that yours has wandered, come back again to body and environment.

The second part of the practice is working with the breath. In this practice rest your attention lightly (yes, lightly) on the breath. Feel it as it comes into your body and as it goes out. There's no special way to breathe in this technique. Once again, we are interested in how we already are, not how we are if we manipulate our breath. If you find that you are, in fact, controlling your breath in some way, just let it be that way. It's a bit tricky to try to be natural on purpose, so don't get caught up in worrying about whether your breath is natural or not. Just let it be however it is.

Again, sit for a few minutes with the posture and the environment and with your breath. In and out. In and out. Sometimes this is quantified as 25% of your attention on your breath. The idea isn't to get it "right," but instead to give you an idea that you're not channeling all of your attention tightly on to your breath. The rest of your attention will naturally be on your body and the environment.

Finally, the last part of the practice is working with thoughts. As you sit practicing, you will notice that thoughts arise. Sometimes there are a great many thoughts, overlapping one over the next: memories, plans for the future, fantasies, snatches of jingles from TV commercials. There may seem to be no gaps at all in which you can catch a glimpse of your breath. That's not uncommon, especially if you're new to meditation. Just notice what happens.

When you notice that you have gotten so caught up in thoughts that you have forgotten that you're sitting in the room, just gently bring yourself back to the breath. You can mentally say "thinking" to yourself as a further reminder of what just happened. This labeling is not a judgment; it is a neutral observation: "Thinking has just occurred." I like to think of it as a kind of weather report: "Thinking has just been observed in the vicinity."

How long should you practice? If you are new to it, try to sit for 10 to 15 minutes and gradually increase to 20 or 30 minutes.

Finally, and perhaps most importantly, remember that mindfulness meditation is about practicing being mindful of whatever happens. It is

NOT about getting ourselves to stop thinking. Repeat: it is not about getting ourselves to stop thinking. It is easy to fall into believing that that is the goal. Many people have a mistaken idea that becoming blank is the goal of meditation. Perhaps it is in some approaches, but it's not in mindfulness meditation. So once again: if you find you are thinking (and you will), include it in what you notice. Don't try to get rid of your thoughts. It won't work, and it's the opposite of the spirit of the practice. We are trying to be with ourselves as we already are, not trying to change ourselves into some preconceived notion of how we ought to be instead.[33]

[32]http://www.dominican.edu/dominicannews/dominican-research-cited-in-forbes-article

[33]https://www.psychologytoday.com/blog/the-courage-be-present/201001/how-practice-mindfulness-meditation

Chapter 6

WHAT IS AGING YOU?

Not enough satisfying social activities

Do you remember being a kid, asking adults how things work? Remember the feelings of amazement and curiosity that you derived from this simple knowledge? Can you recall the joy and excitement that came each morning when you got up out of bed? What will I be doing for fun today? Who will I meet today that could be my new friend? Where is the most fun to be had on a day like today?

It's normal to get bored in life. As we get older, we start to lose joy doing what we used to do, simply because years before, we think we have it all figured out. Now it just seems like we go through the motions; it's almost as if the novelty wore off long ago. Therefore, we begin to lose satisfaction and fall into a rut. We started to take things for granted and predict the outcome on what we read about, hear about, listen to or see on TV. I used to think that I'd look and feel always according to my age and I told myself, you better get used to it. That is the way it is supposed to be.

Many of my friends, neigbours and acquaintances have all sorts of age-related conditions, knee or hip replacements, suffer from inflammation which then restricts them in their daily activities. And when you are hurting in places all the time it makes you not feel good.

We can grow older in years, but it doesn't mean we have to age as fast. And what I mean by this, is that the world is so big and full of interesting experiences, that there is no way that you can say you did it all. There are still so many feats in the world to accomplish, and experience, that life doesn't have to be boring at all. As a matter of fact, you may have your best years still ahead of you. Just imagine, to miss out on one of the best years of your life, just because you feel tired, hurting, exhausted, and limited in what your mind and body can do.

So, what would you want to do, if there were no limitations, if you were able and free to do what you always wanted to do but never attempted? Make it a point to write down some ideas, activities, plans that you'd like to do, some new things you want to try out. Maybe it would be to learn to surf, take a class, or go on a cruise. Write your bucket list! Either way, you're likely to meet someone new out of this, resulting in bonds and friendships to be formed. Or you will learn new concepts and ideas that will alter the way you go about things. Maybe it will make you more appreciative of your current situation, or it will give you the opportunity to do something meaningful for someone else. Maybe you will make a profound discovery that will allow you to contribute in some way, or your experience will make you more compassionate, less prejudiced and more loving towards yourself and others. What if you would miss out on so much? After all, we all have a limited time here on Earth and it is up to each and everyone of us how we want to use the time that is given to us. Doing something new that you never thought you could will give you a tremendous thrill, joy and an uplifting feeling of accomplishment. Why would you not want to experience that?

The first thing people keep telling me is a bunch of excuses. I am too old for that. What would others think of me if I ever did something so outrageous? I do not have the money or I no longer have the physical ability to do this. What if I get hurt, lost, taken advantage of, etc......

Here's the thing, you can come up with as many excuses as you want. Why does the amount of excuses why we cannot do something seem to be limitless? And why do all these limiting beliefs come up when we actually only want to do something we'd love to do?

Using the mindfulness technique I shared with you in the previous chapter, you can get rid of your limiting beliefs and only listen to your heart. Put all these limiting beliefs into the white bubble I mentioned, and blow it into the Universe. Then start putting all your energy into finding ways to make your dreams come true.

Here are some other ways that will help you to feel better, have more energy, keep a clear mind, and stay fit so the sky is the limit no matter your age.

Nutritional deficiency

As adults age, they need more nutrients, like protein, vitamin D and calcium, just to name a few, because our body produces less of certain hormones, our metabolism slows down and our telomeres get shorter. Vitamins and minerals are the ingredients for a healthy life; they are supporting your body composition, your immune function, and your brain health. Without them, your body must work harder and eventually take the necessary nutrition from other body parts like your teeth, bones or muscle mass.

Did you know that age-related muscle loss, also known as *sarcopenia*, begins as early as your 30th birthday? Registered Dietitian and Nutrition Communication Specialist Lindsay Gnant M.Sc., RDN. explains how sarcopenia isn't something that happens overnight, but gradually over time. "But the good news is that no matter your age you can take steps right now to improve your muscle health," says Lindsay.[34]

Beginning around age 30, we start to lose muscle and gain body fat every year. Specifically, age-related muscle loss occurs at an average rate of three to five percent per decade between the ages of 30 and 60 and accelerates significantly after age 60.[35a] This is a serious concern since abnormally low muscle mass, known as sarcopenia, is linked to loss of strength and mobility, culminating in unhealthy aging and frailty.

The good news is that no matter your age, you can take steps to improve your muscle health. Both good nutrition and regular exercise are essential to maintaining muscle mass over time. If you want to give your muscles the best support, these are three steps you can take today to boost your muscles now and in the future.

1. Focus on Protein

Dietary protein is essential for ensuring muscle health. A number of studies have shown that people who consume higher amounts of protein over time, maintain more muscle mass compared to those who consume less protein.[35b] Consuming enough protein-rich foods every day is important, but scientific studies have shown that the source of protein also matters when it comes to preventing age-associated muscle loss. For example, numerous scientific studies support whey protein as the best source of protein to promote muscle building for people of all ages.[35c] Additionally, scientific studies suggest timing of protein intake is important and that dividing your protein intake evenly throughout the day creates an ideal environment for maintaining and building muscle.[35d] So, your best strategy is to choose a balanced amount of protein at each meal and make sure you include a quality source of whey protein on a regular basis.

2. Get Your Vitamin D

It has long been known that vitamin D is important for healthy bones, but continued research has also identified a role for vitamin D in muscle function. In several recent studies, researchers found that vitamin D supplements supported improved muscle strength and balance for older adults.[35e] Surprisingly, one third of all U.S. adults have low levels of vitamin D, or vitamin D insufficiency.[35f] For people who live in southern latitudes, moderate daily sun exposure can help your body make its own vitamin D, but people who live outside of the sun belt or who spend most of their time indoors are at increased risk of suboptimal vitamin D concentrations. Consuming fortified foods and supplementing with vitamin D are more reliable approaches to adequately meeting your body's vitamin D needs.

3. **Resist Muscle Loss With Resistance Exercise**
Regular exercise is one of the most important strategies for maintaining strong, lean muscle. Any type of physical activity has benefits for muscle health, but resistance exercise, such as lifting weights, is more effective for increasing muscle mass and strength.[35g] Regardless of your level of fitness, adding resistance exercise three days per week will have great benefits for both protecting and building muscle.

Better together

Each of these tips for boosting muscle health can have great benefits on its own. However, the results of a recent study published in the *American Journal of Clinical Nutrition* demonstrates that all three work together to produce combined benefits.[35h]

In this study, researchers developed a program to help improve muscle health in older adults who had low muscle mass. The researcher's program evaluated the use of whey protein, vitamin D supplements, and strength training exercises compared to a group of subjects who only exercised. The exercise-only group showed some improvement in muscle health; however, the group following the combined exercise and nutrition program showed significantly greater improvements in muscle health and added more than three pounds of muscle on average over the course of the 12-week study.

Muscle loss is a gradual process with effects that accumulate over time. To stop negative effects of muscle loss, it's important for people of any age to take steps to support muscle health with sound nutrition and regular exercise. Especially when used together, whey protein, vitamin D and strength training can combine to give your muscles a boost.

To slow down the aging process, it is crucial to continue following a diet that is rich in vitamins and minerals. Dark leafy greens, for example, are rich in iron, and help to create healthy red blood cells. And although they are not a substitute for the nutrients found in food, supplements can provide your body further nourishment. Multivitamins usually supply your body with 100% of the most important nutrients.

Telomeres

Since their discovery more than 75 years ago by the Nobel Laureate geneticist Hermann Müller, telomeres have attracted worldwide attention among scientists investigating the aging process.

Telomeres are the protective caps on the ends of chromosomes composed of short DNA sequences protecting our DNA and genetic material from damage. Another Nobel Laureate, Elizabeth Blackburn, likened telomeres to the little plastic caps on the ends of shoelaces (aglets).

Under normal conditions, when a cell divides, telomeres shorten. If they grow too short, they reach what's known as the Hayflick limit (named after the esteemed gerontologist Leonard Hayflick), and the protective capacity of the telomere decreases. Real-world relevance of telomere shortening can be observed during the aging process in humans when comparing the length of telomeres from newborns (8,000 base pairs) to adults (3,000 base pairs) to elderly individuals (1,500 base pairs).

Therefore, because several disease states and pathological processes have been linked to telomere shortening, several academic laboratories and companies have explored intervention strategies to slow down the rate of telomere attrition.

Several lifestyle factors can also significantly affect telomere health and the rate of telomere shortening. Among the most studied factors associated with shorter telomeres are psychosocial: depression, anxiety, and childhood adversity.[35i,j] Other lifestyle factors associated with telomere length include smoking, physical activity, drugs and toxins, and oxidative stress. Indeed, the decades of research implicating oxidative stress in the aging process has recently begun addressing and demonstrating a similarly deleterious role of oxidative stress on telomere length.[35k,l,m] As a result, antioxidant intake and subsequent plasma concentrations may be newly emerging biomarkers of telomere status.[35n,o,p]

Basically, bad things happen when telomeres get short. We addressed already several strategies in this book that will help you to slow down the aging process. Here is a quick overview again:

Slows Down Aging:

- Meditation and practicing Mindfulness
- A healthy diet rich in Omega 3 fatty acids, Antioxidants, Vitamin D
- Sunscreen with UVA and UVB protection
- Exercise
- Be Happy
- Telomeres supporting botanicals
- Regular detoxification/intermittent fasting

Speeds Up Aging:

- Obesity
- Psychological Stress
- UV radiation

- Smoking
- Pollution/Toxins
- Disease
- Oxidative Stress

Oxidative stress is defined as an overabundance of reactive oxygen species (ROS). Excessive oxidative stress damages DNA, proteins, and lipids. While ROS are produced under normal conditions, oxidative stress occurs under conditions of poor health. To prevent oxidative stress, the body requires antioxidant nutrients such as glutathione precursors like the amino acid cysteine along with specific enzymes. [35q,r] Among these antioxidant enzymes is catalase, which functions to convert toxic and DNA-damaging hydrogen peroxide ($H2O2$) into water. [35s,t]

If you suspect that you may be malnourished, let your doctor know. Malnutrition is easy to determine by performing a blood test. However, there may also be several symptoms that develop with a lack of nutrients, .such as brittle hair and nails, receeding bleeding gums, fatigue, and irritability. These are your body's ways of rationing nutrients to supply to the vital organs, while sacrificing other parts of your body. The human body is truly an amazing instrument that will stop at nothing to continue to survive, but at the cost of your energy and livelihood. It is important to follow a diet that provides your body all the nutrients it needs daily, so you may continue to feel your best. [36]

Toxins

No matter how much we try to avoid it, toxins are everywhere. They are either man-made or naturally generated, meaning they occur in the human body, in the foods we consume, the air we breathe, the water we drink, the personal care poducts we use, and even the clothes we wear. They're impossible to avoid. As we get rid of toxins, we feel the "brainfog" dissipate, our skin starts to glow with less impurities, our energy improves, and inches start to melt away.

The body's way of ridding itself of toxins is by excreting them. Every second, we shed off toxins, which are released through the liver into our blood stream and then are flushed out through our kidneys. By drinking more water we help our body to detoxify more easily. Although this is a regular part of life, a buildup of toxins is proven to have adverse effects, and consequently accelerates the aging process.Over time, toxins in your body have the propensity to accumulate. Your liver trie to detoxify but if you are not providing it with the nutritional support and necessary water intake it will place the toxins in fat cells to protect your inner organs. Accumulation of toxins also forces your body to work harder to achieve a perfect homeostasis; because of the many toxins in your body, it has to put in more effort to continue functioning normally. This is what causes you to feel tired all the time. You begin to develop muscle aches and pains as your body strains to function amidst the toxin build-up.[36]

The body becomes more acidic rather than alkaline. An acidic body allows inflammation of all kinds to reduce your quality of life.

I practice nutritionally supported intermittent fasting to give the liver a break and support liver and kidney function which helps my body to detoxify. Intermittent fasting resets, normalizes your body functions and reverts your body back into an alkaline state if practiced on a somewhat regular regime.

The first thing you'll notice after a day or two of intermittent fasting is that any brain fog dissipates, you sleep better during the night and have more energy during the day. It also promotes weight loss, particularly visceral fat around your midsection. Intermittent fasting also promotes telomeres health and thus supportst healthy aging.

According to Dr. Marco Ruggiero, intermittent fasting also promotes and supports brain health. You can learn more about that by listening to his lectures on YouTube about Alzheimer's and Brain Aging. [37][38]

As we age, it is normal to feel more sluggish. We find that we no longer have the ability to run as far as we used to, or lift as much weight as we did back in college. As a result of growing older, we "slow" down to conserve energy.

To combat aging, to stop moving is perhaps one of the worst things you could do. Our bodies were meant to stay in motion. Our hearts were meant to beat strong, and our muscles were meant to fatigue. Part of the process of getting in shape is to break down and rebuild again, yet as we get older, our bodies begin to lose the ability of doing so, unless we begin to take action.

Exercise is for everybody. This doesn't mean you have to begin training for an ultramarathon, but the key is to work at your own pace. So get your heart pumping and begin to feel the oxygen-rich blood as it courses through your capillaries, delivering energy directly to you. The rush in energy should make you want to keep at it, which slows down the aging process as we learned earlier.

Staying active has been proven to increase metabolism. As we get older, our metabolisms plummet. In your 20s, you can eat a donut and it will pretty much go right through you. It seems like it's instantly converted into energy. However, the aging process causes your metabolism to slow down; it's part of the natural cycle. If you ate that same donut in your 50s, you would notice the repercussions on your hips and thighs. Because your metabolism does not allow food to be processed into energy as quickly, that donut most likely turns into adipose tissue, unless you are physically active.

Exercise also ensures that your muscles stay toned. Another normal feature of aging, muscle tone begins to decrease as you get older. However, if you exercise, you can still have those amazing lats and abs well into your 90s!

Your muscles will need energy to work effectively. The more muscle you have, the more energy you'll need. Therefore, your metabolism will correspond to your body's energy demands that are caused by exercise. No longer will you have to be super-cautious of how much you eat. Now, I'm not saying that you should pack yourself with pasta; you should definitely take portioning into account, but by increasing your intake of good protein and complex carbs with exercise, you will begin to feel energised once again.

Portion control is not nearly as important as the quality of the food you eat and its nutritional value. With the right nutrition in combination with the occasional intermittent fasting routine for a day or two, you are less likely to experience cravings and your stomach will start to shrink over time, meaning you will lose the ability to eat huge portions and consume smaller meals more frequently. In short, eat wisely, and keep this in mind:

Every 35 days your skin replaces itself. Your liver needs about a month. Your brain needs a year or more. Your body makes new cells for your body from the food you eat. What you eat literally becomes you. So you are what you eat. You decide what you are made of.

Many people are drawn to the idea that we should be able to consume all of our essential nutrients from whole foods alone, and although this may be a worthy ideal, it's not as easy as it sounds. Although broccoli, spinach, and milk are all calcium-rich, most people don't consume enough of these foods on a daily basis to meet the appropriate recommended daily allowance levels.

Even though studies have conclusively shown that adequate calcium consumption is essential for optimal health, a recent study has shown that people worldwide are still not meeting their daily needs. A recent study conducted by the International Osteoporosis Foundation surveyed almost 7,000 individuals from 80 countries using a calcium calculator. The study estimated these individuals' dietary calcium intake and found on average that the daily intake was less than 600 milligrams per day—far less than the recommended daily allowance. [39]

Many physicians like mine recommend to supplement daily, especially if you are over 50 years old. What I found as a mother and grandmother, though, is that children and young adults these days eat even less nutritious food than their parents.

Here are some key nutrients with scientific evidence that support and accelerate our metabolism as we age in a very gentle yet effective way. Unless we always eat the right amounts of botanicals and other protein sources, we may have to supplement. What I found, though, is that it is almost impossible for most people, including myself, to do so. That is why I supplement to boost my metabolism daily.

Niacin is a B vitamin (B5) with an essential role in the proper function of metabolism and converting food to energy. [39a]

Chromium is an essential trace mineral that supports proper carbohydrate, protein, and fat metabolism. One of its main functions is helping to potentiate the action of insulin in the regulation of blood sugar. [39b,c]

Green tea leaf extract (decaffeinated) contains active compounds, including epigallocatechin gallate (EGCG), which is shown in multiple studies to boost thermogenesis and fat metabolism. [39d,e,f]

Apple cider vinegar is shown in studies to assist with management of blood sugar,[39g,h] although through a different mechanism than chromium. The active ingredient of vinegar is acetic acid, which is also the reason why vinegar has such a pungent taste.

Cayenne pepper contains capsinoids, which are shown to stimulate thermogenesis and that may help curb appetite. [39i,j]

Cocoa seed extract helps modulate fat metabolism through its action on fatty acid synthesis and transport systems.[39k] It may also enhance thermogenesis mechanisms in the liver and adipose tissue to support fat burning. [39l,m]

Not enough sleep

Sleep is crucial to healthy functioning, in all areas of your life. When you sleep, your brain creates new pathways and resets each night. This leads to better retention of information learned. A good night's sleep improves your memory and emotional health. It also allows your body the chance to recycle dead cells and generate new ones. Your inanimate state during deep slumber saves energy that your body needs to repair itself, so you don't feel fatigued during the day. Sleep is basically your body's way of preparing for the day ahead. A good night's sleep for an adult is 6-8 hours a night, 9 if you're an overachiever.

Sleep deprivation prevents you from living a happy, healthy life. Your body can only expend so much energy to keep everything functioning, as well as replacing the millions of body cells that die every day. This can't happen if you don't give your body the chance to rest at night. Furthermore, not allowing yourself to catch some Z's can manifest potentially deadly results.

Look at Joe Truckdriver, for example. He drives trucks for a living, which involves long nights on the road, coffee and lots of caffeine supplements. If he only catches two hours of sleep at a rest stop and continues driving for the rest of the night, his brain might inhibit what's called microsleep. This is a defence mechanism his body executes when it senses sleep deprivation. This phenomenon causes Joe to drift to sleep for a few seconds with his eyes wide open, while his brain basically forces him to fall asleep! At this point, memory cannot be stored. He could be driving for hundreds of miles and not remember a thing. Although Joe Truckdriver may feel he is capable to continue driving, his brief periods of microsleep can cause him to eventually lapse into a deep sleep!

In this scenario, Joe on the road is just as dangerous as a drunk driver. In his sleep-deprived state, he lacks the judgment to make sound decisions, and his brain, in all its confusion, is consequently unfit to drive. By driving tired, Joe is putting other lives, as well as his own, at risk.

Don't be like Joe Truckdriver. Your body, mind, and spirit is dependent on sleep to retain good physical, mental, and spiritual health. If you make time to get at least 8 hours of sleep a night, you will wake up feeling refreshed and energized.

As we get older many of us may experience problems falling asleep or wake up in the middle of the night and have trouble going back to sleep easily. This may be related to depleted melatonin levels.

Melatonin is a hormone made by the pineal gland, a small gland in the brain. Melatonin helps control your sleep and wake cycles. Very small amounts of it are found in foods such as meats, grains, fruits, and vegetables. You can also buy it as a supplement.

As we get older our body produces less of this hormone. If you are working shifts or are under a lot of stress your melatonin production may be out of sync. That is when supplementing may help you to get the sleep you need when you need it.

Your body has its own internal clock that controls your natural cycle of sleeping and waking hours. In part, your body clock controls how much melatonin your body makes.

Normally, melatonin levels begin to rise in the mid- to late evening, remain high for most of the night, and then drop in the early morning hours.

Light affects how much melatonin your body produces. During the shorter days of the winter months, your body may produce melatonin either earlier or later in the day than usual. This change can lead to symptoms of seasonal affective disorder (SAD), or winter depression.

Natural melatonin levels slowly drop with age. Some older adults make very small amounts of it or none at all.

Not getting enough sleep speeds up the aging process, slows down your metabolism, affects your immune function and also influences your brain's health over time.

Dr. Michael Colgan is one of the world's leading scientists on athletic performance and the inhibition of aging.

In his book *Sound Sleep,* Dr. Michael Colgan, PhD states that "on average US and Canadian citizens today get less than 7 hours of sleep a night. It's generally not enough." Besides an increased potential for accidents, brain fog, and a link to cardiovascular health, lack of sleep causes a decline in immune function and can cause pain such as busy leg syndrome, chronic daytime neck and back pain, and a host of other physical complications. More than 90 million Americans suffer from lack of sleep. The effects of sleep deprivation worsen for those over age 40. More than half of Americans over the age of 65 have a sleep-related problem.

Lack of sleep affects our hormone function, like the human growth hormone, which helps with repair during sleep. And believe it or not, but because a lack of sleep increases cortisol levels you will have a hard time maintaining a healthy weight or even losing weight if you have to.

The three most important health functions of sleep, according to Dr. Colgan, are:

1. Memory Consolidation
2. Cellular Repair
3. Brain Development

As well as seven other essential sleep functions like calcium retention in our bones, increase of muscle mass, improved liver function and more.

Everyone who travels a lot, especially to different time zones, may have to increase their melatonin levels temporarily. Astronauts use it while in space to maintain cognitive function, dexterity and decision-making.

Athletes in particular are very sensitive to jet lag. Even a 3 hour time difference between Los Angeles and New York, for example, can already cause a sharp decline in their performance. According to Dr. Colgan, most top trainers in the world use melatonin to level the playing field for their travelling athletes today.

Toxic body

As mentioned previously, toxins have become an inescapable part of our everyday lives. In the previous decade there have been roughly 100,000 different chemicals used in the United States. They're used commercially in the food we eat, the medicine we take, and general house care products that appear completely innocent.

Studies by the Environmental Working Group recently discovered that even unborn babies can't avoid pollution in our toxin-laden society. They found traces of more than 200 commercial chemicals within the umbilical cords before birth. You might not be able to avoid the toxins, but knowing where they come from and how to treat them will help reduce the impact of toxicity significantly.

Signs that you have too many toxins in your body

At this point we know how prevalent toxins are in our society. What we haven't covered is how to tell whether or not the amount of toxins is affecting your overall health in a negative way. Listed below are a few of the most common signs of too much toxin exposure.

- Sleep disorders like insomnia and restlessness
- Body odor and foul breath
- Persisting exhaustion
- Worsening inflammatory problems like arthritis and asthma
- Trouble with digestion
- Development of ulcers or hemorrhoids
- Increase in acne, psoriasis, eczema, and other skin conditions
- Loss of mental clarity and motivation
- Muscle and joint pain
- Worsened PMS symptoms
- Congestion

It's worth noting that these signs are quite general. Some might be a symptom of a completely irrelevant medical condition. Before you assume that your body is polluted, you should always check with your physician.

This is a factor that goes both ways, however. Some physicians might have trouble assigning a source to symptoms caused by body toxicity. They may also attribute the symptoms to something that isn't actually affecting you. This pitfall exists because many medical practitioners aren't required to be well-versed in body toxicity knowledge.

There are also many diseases that can be worsened with body toxicity. Parkinson's, Alzheimer's, depression, cancer, fibromyalgia, and heart disease are all catalyzed with the introduction of toxins.

It's always better to be safe than sorry and take steps to enhance detoxification. The strongest weapon in the fight against body toxicity is knowledge. Reducing your exposure to toxins and practicing detoxification can only encourage a healthier and happier lifestyle.

Major sources of toxins

The first toxin source you should be weary of is food. This plays a huge role in detoxing your body because it is the most direct intake of industrial chemicals. Processed foods are the most common source of additives and chemicals, and should be avoided when possible. Pesticides sprinkled on to crops can also add foreign toxins to your body.

Another deceiving source of toxins is personal care products. Chemicals are abundant in a lot of the shampoo, body wash, soap, lotion, toothpaste, skin cream, and deodorant that we use so casually on a daily basis. If you want to avoid these toxins you can make your own natural healthcare products. Or at least avoid products that contain phthalates and paraben, as there is scientific evidence that they may cause cancer and other health problems. Read the ingredient list; you owe it to your health!

The third major contributor of toxin intake is environmental factors. Inside of your home there could be chemicals lingering from the use of cleaning products, your drywall, carpet or mattresses and a lack of air circulation. Outside of your home there are plenty of pollutants from second-hand smoke, smog, vehicles, and the production of commercial goods.

Keep in mind that these are just some major contributors to toxicity within your body. There are plenty of other small ways that toxins can sneak into your routine. Always exercise caution when purchasing products and carefully examine the areas that you live in.

Easy steps for optimal detoxification

1. **Reduce Exposure** – The first and most obvious step to take is modifying your routine to reduce your exposure to the chemicals. Analyze the sources listed above and try to minimize the pollution you encounter throughout the day. You can start by avoiding these most toxic food ingredients and avoiding these fake foods.

2. **Stay Hydrated** – Water is an essential tool for your body to flush out the chemicals you are exposed to. Purchase a filter to make sure your water is pure and make sure you drink it in regular intervals. A minimum of 8-10 cups of water per day is recommended.

3. **Go Organic** – Switch up that shopping list and ditch the processed foods. Look for organic sources of fruit and vegetables and try to avoid retailers that mass produce them. This will decrease the presence of chemical fertilizers and pesticides that are used for commercial gain. Green vegetables and most fruits have effective detoxifying qualities.

4. **Maintain Healthy Digestion** – Get the right amount of fiber in your diet and make sure that you use the bathroom regularly. The average person should move their bowels one to two times each day to prevent toxin buildup. You can make your own digestive detox smoothie. Probiotics also promote gut health and support regularity. They can be found in fermented foods such as certain yoghurts, kefir, kombutcha, sauerkraut, or kimchi for example.

5. **Exercise** – Getting active will fire up your circulation and turn your body into a toxin flushing machine. Going for runs, swimming, playing sports, or simply getting out to walk around once in a while will help keep you in shape and away from body toxicity.

6. **Supplementation** – There are health supplements out there that will help you reduce toxicity within your body. For example: spirulina and chlorella are two kinds of blue-green algae that are effective at binding and removing toxins from your body, and they work well for detoxing from heavy metal exposure. If you have been exposed to a large amount of toxins and want a quick fix, some recommend taking activated charcoal. Always check with your doctor before taking any supplements.[40]

I use Cleanse For Life from Isagenix, a nutritional supplement that contains a plethora of detoxifying botanicals like aloe, licorice root, turmeric, a blend of specific berries and peppermint, to name a few. It tastes great and is convenient.

[34]http://www.isagenixhealth.net/fight-back-muscle-loss/

[35a]Melton LJ 3rd, Khosla S, Riggs BL. Epidemiology of sarcopenia. Mayo Clin Proc. 2000 Jan;75 Suppl:S10-2

[35b] Houston DK, Nicklas BJ, Ding J, Harris TB, Tylavsky FA, Newman AB, Lee JS, Sahyoun NR, Visser M, Kritchevsky SB; Health ABC Study. Dietary protein intake is associated with lean mass change in older, community-dwelling adults: the Health, Aging, and Body Composition (Health ABC) Study. Am J Clin Nutr. 2008 Jan;87(1):150-5 .

[35c]Wall BT, Cermak NM, van Loon LJ. Dietary protein considerations to support active aging. Sports Med. 2014 Nov;44 Suppl 2:S185-94.

[35d]Areta J, Burke L, Ross M, et al. Timing and distribution of protein ingestion during prolonged recovery from resistance exercise alters myofibrillar protein synthesis. J Physiol. 2013;591:2319–2331

[35e]Muir SW, Montero-Odasso M. Effect of vitamin D supplementation on muscle strength, gait and balance in older adults: a systematic review and meta-analysis. J Am Geriatr Soc. 2011 Dec;59(12):2291-300.

[35f]Cianferotti L, Marcocci C. Subclinical vitamin D deficiency. Best Pract Res Clin Endocrinol Metab. 2012;26:523-537.

[35g]Landi F, Marzetti E, Martone AM, Bernabei R, Onder G. Exercise as a remedy for sarcopenia. Curr Opin Clin Nutr Metab Care. 2014 Jan;17(1):25-31.

[35h]Rondanelli M, Klersy C, Terracol G, Talluri J, Maugeri R, Guido D, Faliva MA, Solerte BS, Fioravanti M, Lukaski H, Perna S. Whey protein, amino acids, and vitamin D supplementation with physical activity increases fat-free mass and strength, functionality, and quality of life and decreases inflammation in sarcopenic elderly. Am J Clin Nutr. 2016 Feb 10.

Puterman E et al. Determinants of telomere attrition over 1 year in healthy older women: stress and health behaviors matter. Mol Psychiatr 2014 Jul 29. doi: 10.1038/mp.2014.70. [Epub ahead of print].[35i]

Shalev I et al. Stress and telomere biology: a lifespan perspective. Psychoneuroendocrinology 2013;38:1835-42.[35k]

Correia-Melo C et al. Telomeres, oxidative stress and infl ammatory factors: partners in cellular senescence? Longev Healthspan 2014;3:1. doi: 10.1186/2046-2395-3-1.[35k]

Demissie S et al. Insulin resistance, oxidative stress, hypertension, and leukocyte telomere length in men from the Framingham Heart Study. Aging Cell 2006;5:325-30.[35l]

Salpea KD et al. Association of telomere length with type 2 diabetes, oxidative stress and UCP2 gene variation. Atherosclerosis 2010;209:42-50.[35m]

Xu Q et al. Multivitamin use and telomere length in women. Am J Clin Nutr 2009;89:1857-63. [35n]

Tiainen AM et al. Leukocyte telomere length and its relation to food and nutrient intake in an elderly population. Eur J Clin Nutr 2012;66:1290-4.[35o]

Paul L. Diet, nutrition and telomere length. J Nutr Biochem 2011;22:895-901.[35p]

Cutler RG. Oxidative stress and aging: catalase is a longevity determinant enzyme. Rejuvenation Res 2005;8:138-40.[35q]

Schriner SE et al. Extension of murine life span by overexpression of catalase targeted to mitochondria. Science 2005;308:1909-11.[35r]

Woo SR et al. Cells with dysfunctional telomeres are susceptible to reactive oxygen species hydrogen peroxide via generation of mul tichromosomal fusions and chromosomal fragments bearing telomeres. Biochem Biophys Res Commun 2012;417:204-10.[35s]

Linn S. DNA damage by iron and hydrogen peroxide in vitro and in vivo. Drug Metab Rev 1998;30:313-26.(35t)

[36]https://www.youtube.com/watch?v=cq_-b77Dkzs

[37]http://www.webmd.com/healthy-aging/features/nutrition-aging-7-signs-inadequate-nutrition

[38]http://www.mindbodygreen.com/0-13737/7-signs-you-have-too-many-toxins-in-your-life.html

[39](http://www.dairyreporter.com/Ingredients/More-calcium-needed-in-diets-Study)

[39a]Gropper et al. Advanced Nutrition and Human Metabolism. Blemont, CA: Cengage Learning, 2009;5:334-337.

Anderson et al. Kuiper et al. Elevated intakes of supplemental chromium improve glucose and insulin variables in individuals. Diabetes 1997;46:1786-91.

[39b]J Trace Elem Med Biol 2011;25:149-53. Hursel et al. The effects of green tea on weight loss and weight meaintenance: a meta-analysis. Int J Obes 2009;33:956-61.

[39c]Dulloo et al. Efficacy of a green tea extract rich in catechin polyphenols and caffeine in increasing 24-h energy expenditure and fat oxidation in humans. Am J Clin Nutr 1999;70:1040-5.

[39d]Hursel et al. Green tea catechin plus caffeine supplementation to a high-protein diet has no additional effect on body weight maintenance after weight loss. Am J Clin Nutr 2009;89:822-30.

[39e]Ostman et al. Vinegar supplementation lowers glucose and insulin responses and increases satiety after a bread meal in healthy subjects. Eur J Clin Nutr 2005;59:983-8.

[39f]Johnston CS et al. Examination of the antiglycemic properties of vinegar in healthy adults. Ann Nutr Metab 2010;56:74-9.

[39g]Ohnuki K et al. CH-19 sweet, a non-pungent cultivar of red pepper, increased body temperature and oxygen consumption in humans. Biosci Biotechnol Biochem 2001;65:2033-6.

[39h]Galgani JE and Ravussin E. Effect of dihydrocapsiate on resting metabolic rate in humans. Am J Clin Nutr 2010;92:1089-93.

[39i]Yoneshiro et al. Nonpungent capsaicin analogs (capsinoids) increase energy expenditure through the activation of brown adipose tissue in humans. Am J Clin Nutr 2012; 95:845-50.

[39j]Matsui N, Ito R, Nishimura E et al. Ingested cocoa can prevent high-fat diet-induced obesity by regulating the expression of genes for fatty acid metabolism. Nutrition, 2005;21(5):594-601.

[39k]Watanabe N, et al. Flavan-3-ols fraction from cocoa powder promotes mitochondrial biogenesis in skeletal muscle in mice. Lipids Health Dis, 2014

[40]http://www.healthyandnaturalworld.com/top-signs-your-body-is-toxic-and-what-to-do-about-it/

Chapter 7

RELATIONSHIPS

LOVE and care for yourself first so that you can love and care for others effectively

What is love?
According to Merriam Webster there are 9 different meanings for love. To me, love is a feeling of affection, kindness, respect and admiration for someone. That someone can also be you!

Love towards another person is the sense of an unselfish loyal and benevolent concern and in that sense it is unconditional. No matter the situation or how that other person behaves and reacts, if we truly love we will not judge but understand.

Love makes us feel good. We all want to be loved. All of us were born with love in our heart. The first people we usually love are our parents or the people who care for and about us.

Love is contagious. If we are loved it is easy for us to love that person back. Sometimes we cannot understand why we feel a fondness for someone. It may start with us taking an interest in someone else, and by getting to know that person we recognize commonalities, similar values, the same sense of humor, or having that sense of being understood without having to explain yourself all the time. Being loved makes it easy for us to share our love with others too. Love is the most precious feeling there is.

Where love is missing it gives room easily to hate, jealousy, and other forms of negativity.

Love is what we feel when we are truly happy with others. Love never leaves although it can be lost for a while. Love is understanding and demonstrating the willingness to work with what you have, vowing to make things better. Love is happiness and positivity. It is the strongest, most benign force in the universe. Everything done in or with love has more meaning for us; it is lasting and will always be remembered.

Do you need others to feel love? Not always, but love is something that needs to be shared and projected on others or on causes to make the best use of it.

Love comes from within. The love you feel is the love you project on others. You can think of love as a tidal wave. If you feel good about yourself or something, and are genuine about your feelings, others can tell. The good vibrations rub off on people, making others feel the happiness you have. And since love and positivity are contagious, why would you want to keep it to yourself? Love wants to be expressed in some way. Love is the perfect antidote to all the negativity we hear about or experience throughout our life. It is healing and helps us to overcome. That is why normally love is only lost for a while until you find it again or it finds you.

Try it. Next time you're in public, smile at somebody. If they smile back at you, it's because they caught your positive feelings, and they are willing to reciprocate. Don't feel bad if they don't smile back, and definitely do not take it personally. It could be that they're facing a battle that they choose to fight on their own, with themselves. But smiling and happiness is contagious, so go out and "infect" others with your good feelings.

You can try and attain perfection by having all the money in the world, but at the end of the day, you always face yourself. Only you will know if you loved what you did and achieved. Remember, no matter where you are in life, no matter who comes and who goes, and what your situation is, there are times when you'll be alone. And it's during these times when you must have enough love for yourself too.

You are in a relationship with yourself for your entire life. There is nobody else in the world, except God, who knows you more than you do. Think of what you are most proud of. Focus on the positive aspects of yourself and everything that makes you special. Remember those times when you were the happiest, and focus on everything that you can influence, shape or create while doing what you love. Doing something out of love is always rewarding.

Marianne Williamson writes in her book *The Law Of Divine Compensation,* "Putting love first means knowing that the universe supports you in creating the good, the holy and the beautiful. It means knowing that you are on earth for a purpose, and that the purpose itself will create opportunities for its accomplishment."

The importance of LOVE in your life

Love is universal. You can apply love to everything, from loving pasta, loving a favourite TV show, to loving your children. This basically means that you are truly grateful that these entities are in your life.

It is crucial that you display gratitude and love in your life, for that is the only thing that will help you to move on and overcome challenges, disappointment, or sadness. There will always be something you can be grateful for in your life, the past year, last month or just yesterday. Maybe you are grateful for the neigbour who helped you out the other day, for the warm weather or the rain that waters your garden. You may be grateful for the victory of your favourite sports team, for the dish you had last night that was so tasty, or the smile someone gave you while you were in line at the cash register in your grocery store. Surely, you will always be able to come up with something that was amazing, felt great, or helped you in some way to feel happy.

Even when you are not feeling well, share that with a friend or loved one and in return you will receive their compassion, understanding or support, which you can be grateful for in return. Let everyone know what you're all about and share what makes you happy. It not only puts you in a good mood, it will also bring events and new people into your life who will add more of what makes you happy. People see you in a good mood, and you will be more approachable because people like positivity.

When I moved 6 years ago into a new neigbourhood I did not know many people. I was constantly looking for ways to meet new people and make more friends in my new community. I love to help others, so I took on volunteer opportunities, and jumped at the offer to host a social circle for other women, who were in a similar situation. Their life had changed because they had moved to this place to retire, their children had grown up and left the home, or they had lost a spouse through separation or death. In short, they all were women looking for new social connections or support in some way. Initially we met for an hour every Monday, but now we usually meet for almost 2 hours, even on holidays. We all have made new friends and the word spreads about how much fun we are all having, so our circle grows steadily. I am grateful for all my sociable sisters, the stories, ideas and opinions they share, and how they have enriched my life in so many ways.

Love is a very strong force. It is merely an affinity to something, but this also portrays your gratitude that whatever you love, exists. Love and gratitude go hand in hand. And when you're reflecting gratitude, life becomes rewarding. You are free to do whatever you love; whatever makes you happy.

Feeling and showing compassion for others

The easiest way of developing compassion for others is to put yourself in their shoes, so you can see their perspective. By doing this, you can try to take their situation and imagine yourself in the same place. Then ask yourself these questions: How would you feel? Would you feel any differently, and why? How would you want people to approach and address you?

The Golden Rule states to "Do unto others as you would have them do unto you." All cultures in the world have this principle in their sacred texts; it has been passed down since the beginnings of recorded writings, such as Hammurabi's Code. What this means, is that you should treat others the way you prefer to be treated. The Golden Rule contains all the ingredients you need to develop compassion for others, which promotes doing good to others using empathy.

Because we are all different and experience things, events and people in different ways, it will certainly help to have respect for the feelings of others and try to understand their point of view. What may be hard for you to do, feel or think, might be easy for someone else, and vice versa. Someone once said "People do not always remember what you said and how you said it, but they will always remember how you made them feel." When we can achieve that, we act out of love and respect, which also creates something someone may be grateful for, and certainly makes everybody happy over-all.

All it takes to understand others is to act toward them as if you were in their situation. Treat them the way you would want to be treated if you were in their shoes. Most likely, they will reciprocate these feelings, which is the basis of love and respect for others. It is a universal law, that the more love, gratitude and compassion we give, the more we will receive.

Showing an interest in other people's life, background, experience and learning from them

People like to talk about themselves. Ask me about my life, and I will ramble on and on, perhaps unable to stop talking until you tell me to. But I enjoy it.

It's fun learning about other people. No two people are alike, so experiences and life stories vary, making things even better. The way to grow close to another person is by hearing their story and talking about their life. By getting their take on things, and their perspectives, you will get people to open up, and learn along the way. Ask them anything to start with. Engage in a conversation by talking about the weather (because honestly, it is something we all have to live with). I love to ask people about their dreams, about what would they love to do if they had the time, and money was of no concern. Learn more about their family, their hobbies, and what they want to accomplish. Nothing gets a person more excited than talking about what they want to do with their lives, because it forces them to focus on their goals.

How does it make you feel when someone shows an interest in what you do or go through, your struggles or the things you love to do? Would you like that? Does that indicate to you that you are somewhat important to that person? Showing an interest in others and their lives makes us all feel valued. To them you become a sounding board and they may ask you for your opinion or your advice, or just let you know how they feel about themselves, their current situation or the things they are involved in. To you, the listener, what they have to say may be of value. Maybe you will learn something new. Maybe you will realize that you are not the only one who struggles at times and that everyone has challenges to overcome. Maybe you will also take some valuable lessons from what you hear so you can apply them in your own life. Connecting with and listening to what people have to say creates value on both sides and helps everyone in some way.

This was and still is an area I want and need to improve on, especially because my passion in life is to help, support and assist others in various ways. How can I effectively do so when I am not prepared to learn first where people are hurting or what they are struggling with? Maybe that other person could also be helpful to me or someone I know, or a collaboration would add value to my offerings. Alone we can only do so much. As a team that brings together different skills, traits and ideas we can achieve so much more in a shorter time.

Being open to make new connections and developing new friendships

A friendship is one of the greatest gifts in the world. It answers a primal need to belong to a pack, to another human being. Developing a friendship is a very beautiful thing, and it may take some effort. Friendship is sometimes made up of selfless sacrifices because you care about that person enough to always be there for them when they need you. It also means that you are open enough and honest enough to ask them for support when you need it. In a friendship there is always enough trust and love for the other so misunderstandings or mistakes can always be forgiven or made up for. Other times, one friend might not understand why his brother acts the way he does. But mistakes can be forgiven with time and patience, and the love of a friendship helps to mend things.

True friends know the ins and outs of each other. They are close like brothers and sisters, to the point that they consider each other family. It gets to the point where they can confide in one another, and because of them, things get better.

However, it does not start off like that. It is a little strange to act chummy to somebody you don't know. You risk being turned away. How you want to introduce yourself is entirely up to you, and I trust that you know how to spark a conversation.

First of all, you have to figure out what you like. Is it sports? Art? Are you a movie buff? In your spare time, take the liberty of pursuing whatever you want to do. Go to a football game. Join an art club or a bowling team. This will help you attract people with similar interests.

Now I'm not saying that this will automatically happen. The key is not to try too hard, and let things happen naturally. Attracting a friend is somewhat like attracting a potential date; you should be wary of how you come across.

However, you are allowed to make an advance. Introduce yourself and see where things go from there. Smiling always helps too!

If things go well, you are encouraged to start with small talk. Ask them about music, their hobbies, movies, actors and actresses. Don't go straight into politics, death, war, or basically anything considered controversial. These are touchy subjects and you don't exactly know who you're dealing with just yet. Cover the basics first.

There really aren't official "steps" to make friends. You just need to let it happen naturally. All people have different personalities, so you know that all relationships are going to vary by likes, dislikes, and anything in common. But if you are kind and do the right thing by your friend, you can expect to be buddies forever!

Friendship is very precious and valuable, as long as you put your time and dedication into it. Be a good listener and really get to know that person, and give that person the respect they give you. Be a friend and have an open mind. You might learn some new things and make timeless memories.

Sharing own life experiences with others and knowing when to ask for help

Sometimes pride in oneself can be a hard pill to swallow. We feel ashamed to ask for help because we think we can make it in this world all by ourselves. And that's a good thing because it demonstrates self-sufficiency, but what about those times when we are desperate? When we can't go on without a little assistance, a little nudge from our neighbour?

I get a sense of satisfaction by helping others, or else I wouldn't be writing this book to offer advice to you. If you're reading this, I sense that you may be depressed or just going through a rough patch in life. That's alright; we all have been there at some point.

Everyone's lives are different. The way one person lives their life is different from another person's, as they derive their values and beliefs from the experiences in their past. Just by looking at a person, you cannot tell what they have been through. Therefore, it is important to be as nonjudgmental as possible when helping someone in need.

My point is that we all need someone to lean on at some point. And you shouldn't be afraid to ask for help. I've asked for help plenty of times. Throughout the process of receiving help, I've felt ashamed, embarrassed, and disappointed in myself. But without the assistance of other people, I probably wouldn't have gotten this far in life. At the end of the day, I felt better about myself, and grateful for the generosity of others. Because of the situations that have prompted me to ask for help, I feel like I have grown closer to the people who know me. They know my life experiences, and based on that, trust is formed.

Being authentic, having integrity, being trustworthy and trusting in others too. Listening more to your own intuition.

Your gut feeling is your inner conscience trying to tell you something. Your gut doesn't only speak when you're hungry; I'm talking about your own instinct that keeps you out of trouble.

We all know when something is not right. When there is something astray from the baseline, when there is ever a deviation from the norm, our instinct lets us know. This is in no way a paranoia; we aren't crazy, but we know to listen to our hearts when we know that someone isn't to be trusted.

In this modern world, it's hard finding people to trust. We are all so connected, yet so distant. You can see it on the trains, as the majority of people spend most of the time on their phones instead of talking to others. You see it on the news, as acts of violence break out in seemingly the safest of places.

The recent terrorist attacks caused many people to lose trust in each other. Now, nobody knows who's armed and who isn't. Because of all this, we are all afraid that it may happen again. That's why it's important to be transparent. Don't just say you're trustworthy, show it.

Some ways to help people trust you is to be honest and open in communicating with others, acting in a non-violent manner.

This means standing by your word; doing something you said you would do. This means taking the initiative and following through. Nobody respects a person who doesn't communicate to others, because they view him as unreliable, or flaky.

Have integrity in all that you do, even if nobody is watching. More likely than not, someone is watching. Somebody who uses their instincts can read into you; they can tell if you're genuine or not. Being yourself is the most important thing you can be.

Love is all. Some say it is God. Regardless of what you believe, this strongest of all emotions can make your life or bring you grief if it is not returned. Let's talk about that in Chapter 9.

You can overcome all evils, challenges and misfortune with enough love in your life.

Chapter 8

LIFE PURPOSE

Feeling and expressing gratitude regularly regardless of your current circumstances

In the history of the universe, a human life is just a speck on the timeline. The earth itself is slightly over five billion years-old, and yet we've just recently been able to reach the life expectancy of about 80 years.

Life is short, but to human beings, it matters. The short time we have on this earth is spent pondering how to navigate through the years. Some get a little lost and end up on the downside of luck. Though life has its ups and downs, some people end up feeling hopeless and in despair during its trials. Unable to make sense of it all, they consider putting it to an untimely end.

How you cope with your current circumstances determines where you end up in the future. Life is about experiences good and bad, learning from them, improving yourself, using your unique skills to help others while accepting their support in return, enjoying all that is good and beautiful and being honest with yourself. Some of us are blessed finding our purpose, which helps to enjoy what we do and how we live our life. Throughout the quest to find your niche, you will come across many ways to think about it. Always look at life positively no matter your circumstance. After all, your life is your gift from God.

Many people, including me some years ago, do not have any idea of their purpose in life. I was passionate about too many things and never really focused on one or two things for a greater impact. Being a parent makes it easier for a while as we focus on our family and children. What about those of you who do not have any children? Maybe you are not even in a long-term relationship. What about those of us who lost a child or our children have grown up? What if you are young and just want to get ahead in life? I never thought about my purpose in life when I was young. I just wanted to experience new things, have fun and enjoy myself.

Elisabeth Gilbert, the author of *Eat, Pray, Love,* always lectured about living your purpose by following your passion until one night she received a message from one of her fans, who pointed out that not everyone has a purpose yet, or at least does not know about their purpose in life. Some are still looking for it and are not even sure that they will ever find it. I love her advice, "Some follow their passion and some follow their curiosity. Release yourself from the pressure and be like the hummingbird that may eventually lead you to your passion."

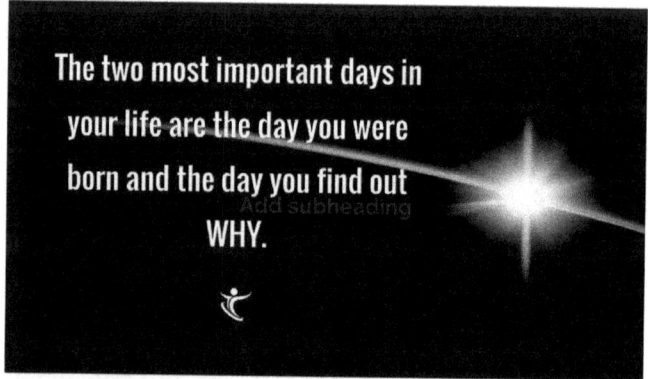

Remain curious to learn about new ideas, experience new places or ways of going about things, see your life as an awesome exciting adventure with the opportunity to try something new, meet new people, see things through their eyes, and expand your horizon. For example, just take a different way home every day, or visit a place you have never been to before. Sometimes we decide to go to a certain place in our area to check it out and then we take a different turn which has lead us to another awesome place we did not even know existed. When you can manage to just be curious and give something a try it may one day lead you to something you will be passionate about. You will feel compelled to share it with others and help more people along the way. Your passion will turn into the purpose for your life.

To look at life positively doesn't mean to be blind-sided by all of the setbacks. You need to understand that life isn't a walk through the victory garden. To approach life with an optimistic view, you need to take whatever comes at you like an educational experience. You learn from all of the situations you're in. If you make a mistake, take away from it and move on.

You should consider that no matter where you are at the moment in your life, this situation is temporary. As time goes by, something is bound to change that will affect where you are. Expect for things to be better. Or maybe worse. But if you want things to be better for you, then think on the brighter side of life. Look at what you have accomplished, and go from there. Maybe to start, be grateful that 13 billion years of the universe's existence has led up to yours!

One thing is certain; you are here for a reason! You are an amazing human being with unique qualities, traits and gifts. Use them and find your purpose in life along the way.

Giving back when you can and accept other people's ways of giving back to you too

Humans are communal animals. We commonly associate with others because we take into account similarities and differences, which we utilize to our benefits. People are selfish, but they are also giving. They will help others because it is morally right, and maybe because of a similar situation they were in before. But first and foremost people help each other because it feels good.

If you need a hand-up at times, you should be readily willing to accept it. The reason behind this is that there have been certain times before that other people have benefitted from you. There were times when people needed help and you were ready to help them, like perhaps at your job, or in a family situation. After you receive help, offer help whenever you're needed. People will never forget a kind person. Some of us are very busy and we may not always realize when, how and what we can help with. Communicating with others and listening to someone's situation is something we all need to work on so we can add more value to our life and make a difference for someone else. Some people may be too proud to ask, or they are afraid to admit to a weakness or situation. So when you think of someone take it as a hint from your spirit to connect and find out how that person is doing. That other person may be surprised yet very grateful for your thoughtfulness and interest in them. You may already do a great service by just listening. Moreover, if you help others, you give your life more purpose. The feeling of being needed, adding value to someone's life or just giving them a hand once will also help you to deepen friendships or create new ones.

Being passionate about and enjoy what you do

In the quest of doing things that feel good, are enjoyable and trigger your curiosity, you'll find something that calls to you. It can be anything in the world. What do you want the world to reflect more of? Peace? Music? Sports? Respect for the environment? Visual, performing or any other form of art? Medicine? Justice? Science? The list goes on.....Fill your world with the things you are fond of and want to learn more about. Developing an affinity for something is constructive, as the more you explore it, the more you will learn about it. It may lead you to getting involved. You will meet like-minded people along the way. Pretty soon, you will become an expert at your hobby, and others will flock to you for advice. You'll want to congregate with like-minded people to learn from them, have fun together working with it or discussing it. Stay open-minded and your passion can become your purpose. You may even change your career. Following your curiosity, your heart makes you feel happy, and in that moment, life is wonderful.

The point in life is not always made clear to everyone, but if you are passionate about what you do, if you have fun, and reflect joy, then the point in life will find you, and that is to seek enjoyment.

Finding true meaning in everyday life i.e. looking for ways to be of service to others

Helping others make their lives better also fills you with a sense of accomplishment. This means that someone put you to use, and put their faith and trust in you to help them solve a conflict, overcome a challenge, lend a hand or just be a listening board. They probably are grateful for your support and value your relationship now even more.

On the other hand, the people you help out may get by easily without you. Perhaps they look to you for your opinion, or your advice or a referral.

Either way you look at this, you are needed, you provide value, you make someone else feel better. And that's a good thing. This person trusted you enough that you could help them. If you fall on hard times, the people you help are grateful enough for you to help you in return. The gratitude that you derive from this will feel great, so you are compelled to help others in need, as your way of giving back to the generous community.

Creating a legacy that will benefit others once we are gone (giving valuable advice, providing education and guidance, creating foundation or charity, gifts for public use etc.)

A unique feature of humanity is the way we approach death. Death is certain for every single person; it is described as the "great equalizer" because nobody, regardless of socioeconomic class, can escape it.

In an effort to be memorialized after death, most of us want to leave something behind, so that we can be remembered in death and therefore not completely gone forever. We strive to create legacies so that our names can go down in history. I look at it this way: "Every person that enters your life leaves a footprint." To me a legacy is something of value that will live on for the benefit of others, even when I am gone. Over time our society has evolved in collective wisdom, through scientific advances, through the curiosity and courage of those before us. This is not only true for advances in technology, but also for the evolvement in humanity, the way we respect and treat others and the environment we live in.

Have you thought about your own death? It's pretty natural to feel afraid about it, but have you thought about what will happen after you're gone? How do you think the world would benefit from you (and not necessarily by your absence, but by you even being on this planet to start with)?

Give your life meaning by loving enough, caring enough, listening enough, communicating enough, and creating great memories along the way. You don't have to try to become a celebrity, but the meaning of having a purpose in life is to make an impact on the life of someone else. Live a life of helping others out with theirs.

Let your spirit shine to inspire, lift others up and look for ways to create positive change in people's lives, and in the world. (Innovation, stewardship of the environment, advancements in science, philanthropy, volunteering etc.)

In this war-torn world, we witness many negative events in a day. On the news, there are always reports of attacks, bombings, and people experiencing the worst in life. Many of us become more frightened, or angry about the injustice and violence we see or hear about. All of us are very different in our opinions and beliefs. As much as we want to, we can't help everyone. There has always been violence and injustice in the world and I look at that as something we can all learn from. As a German citizen I always had to live with the guilt and shame of the cruelty my people have caused on others before and during the second world war. The violence and disrespect for other cultures, feelings, challenges and religions I see today is a constant reminder that there is still a lot to be learned from the past.

You have the potential to shape the world in which you live. It is up to you how you navigate the world you were born into; the world that is part of your life. If you set high goals for yourself, you give yourself something to reach for. Reaching that goal can become your purpose in life. As you get closer to achieving your goal, help others as best as you can along the way, and out of gratitude for being able to reach out to you, they will want to help you in return. This bond of trust can help form lifelong friendships, and therefore fulfill the human need to be part of a group and not alone. The exchange in help speaks volumes; it is never truer that we all need somebody to depend on at some point in our life. It makes life so much more enjoyable, easier and meaningful for all.

We all are able to contribute in some way for the greater good. For example by caring for and raising responsible citizens every parent contributes already to the greater good of society. Others can contribute through volunteer work, by caring for an ailing family member or by getting involved in a political party or movement to improve our life in some way in the future. Everyone working in the educational field, in customer service, in research and development, in a trade …..and the list goes on, everyone who wants to make a difference through their work is contributing in some way or another to the benefit of someone else.

When you are working to the benefit of another person or for better understanding of a certain cause, for more peace, or better quality of life either for money, as a volunteer or a student the future of others will be better because of you.

So let your light shine brightly, live by example and compel others to approach life in a similar way. This is the only way to improve and make our world a better place every day.

Chapter 9

WHAT'S GOT LOVE TO DO WITH IT?

How much do you love yourself?

Love is the key ingredient for a happy life. Throughout the chapters of this book, we've described the true meaning of love, the different types of love, and how it is applied every day. We've also stated that love is generated from within. You must love yourself before you can project it toward others. The actions you have towards others are a direct reflection on how you feel about yourself.

If you do not love yourself, you may not care about your health, your feelings, your precious body and your amazing talents and gifts. You are unsatisfied with your life and you dislike certain aspects of it. You may complain a lot, feel shame, anger or guilt. By feeling unsatisfied, you do not have the room or attention to be grateful for what you have, which can truly help you change your outlook on the life you live. If you want to live a positive life, you have to take care of yourself and be ready to embrace changes and challenges as something to gain from and grow on.

So I ask you, how much do you love yourself? Do you know yourself enough to determine what needs to be changed, if you happen to feel otherwise? Before finishing this book, evaluate where you're at right now. If you love yourself, you will know what you need and how to make life even better. You will feel ready to feel happy.

Sexuality as an extension of love towards your partner

Humans are one of the rare species that can use sex not only as a method of procreation, but a form of affection. Evolution has made sex enjoyable to promote procreation to ensure the survival of the species. During sex, such neurotransmitters like serotonin and oxytocin are released; these chemicals are a few ingredients for bonding, which is a human need. Throughout the evolution of our species, we have learned to form meaningful relationships, and also learned to use sex as a form of affection to those to whom we are attracted.

A romantic relationship, like other relationships, is give and take. This exchange is possible because of love for each other. To show love to one another, a couple uses sexual attraction to portray their affection toward each other. Sex is therefore a form of intimate love.

The feeling of love increases our vibration and energy

Love helps us think positively. Thinking positively is a motivator. It helps you believe and have total trust and confidence that you can achieve what you want to, that your efforts will be successful. This helps you overcome all obstacles to achieving your goals. Think love. Breathe love. Attract what you love into your life, and feel the love of what you do and who you are flow into you.

New York Times bestselling author Masaru Emoto beautifully illustrates in his book *The Hidden Messages In Water* the power of Love and Gratitude through his scientific work with water. Using high speed photography Dr. Emoto discovered that crystals formed in frozen water reveal changes when specific, concentrated thoughts are directed towards them. He found that water from clear springs and water that has been exposed to loving words, shows brilliant, complex, and colourful snowflake patterns. In contrast, polluted water, or water exposed to negative thoughts, forms incomplete, asymmetrical patterns with dull colours. The impact of Dr. Emoto's research create a new awareness of how we can positively impact the earth and our personal health.

Just consider that as humans our body is 60-70% water. Our thoughts and the thoughts of the people around us have a significant impact on how we feel and how healthy we are. Just imagine, if thoughts can do this to water, what will they do to you.

Check out his jaw dropping photography on YouTube https://www.youtube.com/watch?v=tAvzsjcBtx8

Feeling of love and gratitude has an effect on every cell in our body

Love is an affirmative, positive feeling. *Bottom line is, love is the greatest power on the planet and WHEN WE GIVE IT, there's no doubt that confidence is one of its many wonderful by-products, leaving us feeling, doing and giving our best.*

Some reading for you ... While teaching at USC, Dr. Leo Buscaglia was moved by a student's suicide to contemplate human disconnectedness and the meaning of life, and began a non-credit class he called Love 1A. This course became the basis for his first book, titled simply LOVE. His dynamic speaking style was discovered by the Public Broadcasting System (PBS) and his televised lectures earned great popularity in the 1980s. At one point his talks, always shown during fundraising periods, were the top earners of all PBS programs. This national exposure, coupled with the heartfelt storytelling style of his books, helped make all of his titles national Best Sellers; five were once on the New York Times Best Sellers List simultaneously.

Fondly known as The Love Doctor, Buscaglia died of a heart attack on June 12, 1998 at his home in Glenbrook, Nevada, near Lake Tahoe. He was 74.

What follows is a list of Buscaglia's books:

1. *Love (1972)*
2. *The Way of the Bull (1973)*
3. *The Fall of Freddie the Leaf (1982)*
4. *Living, Loving and Learning (1982)*
5. *Loving Each Other (1984)*
6. *Amar a los demás (1985)*
7. *Personhood (1986)*
8. *Bus 9 to Paradise (1987)*
9. *Papa My Father (1989)*
10. *Because I Am Human (1972)*
11. *The Disabled and Their Parents: A Counseling Challenge (1983)*
12. *Seven Stories of Christmas Love (1987)*
13. *A Memory for Tino (1988)*
14. *Born for Love (1992)*[41]

[41]*https://en.wikipedia.org/wiki/Leo_Buscaglia*

Chapter 10

WOMEN UNITED FOR CHANGE (WUFC)

WUFC is a charity I began in March 2015 in order to empower other women through education, training and financial assistance so they can lead a successful life and influence positive change. This charity allows me and the other founding members to create lasting change in the lives of women in underprivileged areas of the world from the ground up. In fact, working through Women United For Change feels like a true blessing and I am deeply honored to be a Founding Member of this powerful initiative.

Please note that a portion of the proceeds from this book will go towards my charity.

An alliance with PCI's **Women Empowered** (WE) program will allow us to maximize our impact and ensure our success through careful monitoring and measurement of progress. As of March 2016 we are sponsoring more than 2,000 women.

PCI's **(Project Concern International)** mission is to prevent disease, improve community health and promote sustainable development worldwide. It is one of the most respected and economical NGOs. The Clinton Foundation, The Bill and Melinda Gates Foundation and organizations like Starbucks have worked with them for years.

Vision

Motivated by our concern for the world's most vulnerable children, families and communities, PCI envisions a world where abundant resources are shared, communities are able to provide for the health and wellbeing of their members, and children and families can achieve lives of hope, good health and self-sufficiency.

Strong Roots

In 1961, a young doctor from San Diego volunteering at a Tijuana clinic saved the lives of two small children who were dying of pneumonia. This experience led Dr. James Turpin to found PCI and forever change the lives of millions of children and families around the world by providing health and hope to those most in need. Since then, the focus of the organization has remained true to its founder: PCI works in vulnerable communities to improve health and create long-term change by helping people help themselves. For 50 years, thousands of dedicated individuals and groups have worked to make this vision a reality.

We believe that women are the solution to poverty and violence. This initiative promotes the economic and social empowerment of women through the formation of self-managed and self-sustaining savings groups. A women's savings group (WE group) consists of 15-20 women who save money together, lend to each other and conduct business together.

By supporting PCI's WE Initiative, you can empower vulnerable women with training and mentoring from a PCI facilitator in literacy, numeracy and small business development as well as social support and individual leadership development enabling them to become powerful agents of their own transformation, and that of their families and communities for a lifetime. **My goal is to empower 100 women every year!**

Why women?

- Women are effective agents of change.
- Women have proven to be a low risk INVESTMENT.
- Women MANAGE meager resources wisely.
- Women PRIORITIZE their decisions based on the needs of their families.
- Women DEVOTE available resources to their children's education and to the productivity of their households.

Results:

- Increased self-confidence, self-determination and self-reliance.
- Increased income and investment in productive activities.
- Increased food security and access to education for children.
- Increased participation in household decision making.

How can you help?

1. Make a donation. Your investment can change the life of:
   - One woman: $50 over an 18 month period
   - One group (15-20 women): $1,000
   - Five groups: $5,000
   - Ten groups: $10,000
   - A community: $25,000
   - A country: $100,000
   - A region: $500,000

2. If you can't make a donation at this point, help me reach my goal by sharing this page on Facebook and Twitter! Or, even better, send an e-mail to friends you think might be interested in contributing and include a link to my page!

Collectively we can accomplish much more! Thank you so much for your generosity!

my.pciglobal.org/ankemayer

www.ingramcontent.com/pod-product-compliance
Lightning Source LLC
Chambersburg PA
CBHW051106160426
43193CB00010B/1339